PREFABRICATED AND MODULAR ARCHITECTURE

Aligning Design with Manufacture and Assembly

PREFABRICATED AND MODULAR ARCHITECTURE

Aligning Design with Manufacture and Assembly

WILLIAM J. HOGAN-O'NEILL

THE CROWOOD PRESS

First published in 2021 by
The Crowood Press Ltd
Ramsbury, Marlborough
Wiltshire SN8 2HR

enquiries@crowood.com
www.crowood.com

British Library Cataloguing-in-Publication Data
A catalogue record for this book is available from the British Library.

ISBN 978 1 78500 806 1

Dedication
To Frieda

Typeset by Simon and Sons
Printed and bound in India by Parksons Graphics

Contents

PREFABRICATED AND MODULAR ARCHITECTURE has been my passion for many years and together with colleagues at HOCA Practice I set about to deliver an alternative approach to the conventional way of practising architecture. I am grateful to colleagues who share a similar commitment to my own.

There are numerous persons who during the preparation of this book were extremely forthcoming with information and to whom I am indebted. I must, however, particularly mention Costi of TRJ Construction Ltd, Shaun Foy of Frame Homes (SW) Ltd, Daniel Walker of Kingspan Timber Solutions Ltd, Chris Tonkin of Structural Timber Projects Ltd, Simon Beale of TMP UK South Ltd, Paul Farrelly of CIMC MBS Ltd, JJ Smith & Co. (Woodworking Machinery) Ltd and Mark Jenkins of Kingspan TEK Building System, all of whom have my sincere gratitude for responding to my questions and providing a wealth of information.

I do not hold a monopoly on passion for prefabricated architecture. My research into historical features on prefabricated housing allowed me to liaise with Jane Hearn of the Prefab Museum, to whom I owe massive thanks for the wealth of information she imparted to me.

I must mention my friend and professional colleague Paddy Doyle, whose energy and commitment to prefabricated and modular buildings are inspirational and with whom I continue to enjoy special occasions discussing matters surrounding the world of prefabrication and modular buildings.

This book would never have been possible without the perseverance and support of my wife Frieda who made space for me to function with ease and who put life on hold until its completion, as well as managing the proofreading regime.

WHEN EXAMINING THE ATTRIBUTES AND constraints associated with prefabricated buildings through panelization or modularization, the discussion usually comes first to housing. Housing shortages have a history dating back to the Industrial Revolution and have remained acute since the start of the twentieth century. This continues today, two decades into the twenty-first century. For many individuals and communities, the impression that prefabrication evokes will centre around housing. There has likewise been an interest in applying prefabrication to health care, education, recreation and similar community projects but none of these stimulates such profound emotions as housing.

Notwithstanding the degree to which current trends demand ever more adherence to economies of scale, sustainability obligations together with ecological challenges, many government departments and housing associations are now seeking to identify how the once more forthright 'system building' ideology of the past could be used in a more compliant manner to satisfy current demands of house buyers, funders and the architectural fraternity's design criteria.

The potential for satisfying many of the pressures associated with education, housing, health needs and similar projects is real and acknowledged by prefabricated projects already completed. Within the British Isles, prefabrication has been less than successful in delivering building solutions over the past decades. This is primarily because of previously held perceptions. For now, prefabricated and modular architecture can only be considered as a 'work in progress' enterprise as a significant

measure of reluctance continues to prevail. Beyond this immediate challenge in prefabrication lies a further vision for exploring current technology and assembly techniques to facilitate high-rise projects where modularization is at their core. Prefabricated and modular architecture continues to forge a space in the minds of some construction professionals more than in architects, albeit at a slow pace, but the indications suggest it is becoming a design specialism that architects should not ignore.

Defining prefabricated and modular architecture can be a very emotive endeavour, not just by how it is identified or referred to but also by the manner in which it is applied in creating buildings. Within the construction industry, one fraternity will maintain that prefabrication, or any product derived from the off-site manufacturing (OSM) process, as not contributing to architecture, but is primarily a process which serves the on-site construction process as its defining purpose. Others attached to the conventional construction ethos might subscribe to OSM as being a vehicle to deliver building projects more quickly, but would prefer not to have to surrender a significantly large sub-contractor package to a specialist manufacturer outside their direct control, potentially impacting on their own overall profitability.

Current thinking within certain design fraternities, too, often sees prefabrication and modular buildings as a particular design and build specialism. It is often viewed as a means primarily to facilitate the architect's overall architectural design or as a convenient vehicle for delivering a specialist sub-contractor design package through the main contractor. Architecture, on the other hand, should be seen as a whole series of considerations for delivering buildings and design solutions of which prefabrication is one. These design considerations are likely to include the following: design where spatial arrangement is considered relative to its intended function; the selection of materials in relation to function or context and locality; the building's robustness relative to climate or intended performance; and the actual site context in relation to its surrounding built environment. All of these embrace the building's architecture. For prefabrication to communicate meaning and status within the building's architecture therefore, architectural design must also embrace the fabrication design of the components with their manufacturing and assembly entities as a natural part of the total architectural design solution for the site. For many centuries, however, methods employed in delivering buildings have been monopolized by conventional on-site hand-built construction practices conforming to familiar customs and procedures. By contrast, within the UK over more recent decades especially, the reliance on past generations of construction methods and preferences is coming under a number of significant challenges on a number of levels. At long last there is a call from government for 'the client's professional team or advisers to adopt a different approach' (House of Lords, 2017–19, p. 30) by enabling off-site manufacture as a means of expediting a change of emphasis from conventional construction to factory manufacturing and industrialization.

This book explores some principal features surrounding prefabrication applications and processes. It will introduce clients, construction professionals, architects and professional designers, students and private individuals to many of the typical core elements surrounding prefabricated and modular architecture and set about debunking the myths associated with prefabricated buildings. A valuable insight of necessary interactions associated with on-site activities and OSM and assembly processes is examined, highlighting what it takes to approach a prefabricated project, whether it is delivered through panelization or modularization. The distinction is made between on-site construction and manufacturing and assembly, and how the manufacturer's installation and assembly processes at the site now seek to substitute for over 90 per cent of the conventional site construction activities. The competition that exists between conventional construction and OSM alternatives remains a formidable stumbling block in the minds of many, but current trends indicate negative perceptions are on the wane, with prefabricated and modular architecture now recognized as a dedicated design and manufacturing specialism.

Chapter One

Prefabrication – Definitions and Explanations

Origins and Early Applications

Nomadic Tent Architecture

Early nomads were among the first engineers and users of prefabrication that we would recognize today. We associate nomadism as a lifestyle of moving from one place to another, suggesting an attentiveness to portability and all the inconveniences associated with such a way of life if compared to life within a settlement. Whilst they were not equipped with the benefits of an industrialized off-site manufacturing (OSM) process that we would recognize today, the solution available for them to provide their mobile home was nonetheless facilitated by a simple kit of parts; namely, a timber-framed structure covered with a patchwork of skins. The assembly process associated with the early nomadic tent was, by and large, similar throughout various regions, although the circular 'plan form' layout and size might have varied within different nomadic cultures and would have evolved further throughout the centuries, even up to the present times. The circular plan form of the *ger* is a natural and obvious choice in exposed locations for the Mongolian nomads of Central Asia as the circular structure has less resistance to wind. Wind and water move naturally around a circular building with greater ease than compared to a square-cornered structure, and our present-day obsession to manage air tightness and water ingress remains omnipresent. Similarly, a rounded roof will facilitate further by preventing 'air-planing' in strong wind conditions which can cause the roof to be torn off a building.

The essence of the traditional Mongolian *ger*, meaning home, or *yurt* in Turkish, extols the epitome of simplicity. They consist of expandable timber lattice wall sections which, when opened up to a given height, form a circular plan arrangement when

Traditional Mongolian *ger* ('yurt' in Turkish).
The *tono*, central piece that forms the nucleus of the family's *ger*.

connected together. Straight timber poles (rafters) form the roof which connects the circular crown to the top of the circular lattice wall structure. The crown, or *tono*, is a special piece of craftsmanship, often handed down from one generation to the next; it forms a central tie at the top of the structure and at the same time, creates a nucleus within the space where the fire for cooking is located, allowing smoke to dispel at high level. This simple building concept is applied even today in recreational enterprises that are located in natural environments deemed to be particularly sensitive, such as forests, ski-huts, wellness and retreat centres and lodge sites. As such they are not considered to be a formation of a built environment as we would describe them in today's context, primarily because these structures are not permanent and can be removed within hours.

For early nomads, mobility remained a prerequisite for exploiting food resources that relied upon tending their livestock at various locations at different times and climatic conditions during the year. Such a way of life dictated the necessity for creating a shelter from the elements and, in some instances, doing this in very severe climatic conditions, varying from extremely cold to excessively hot. One common feature for nomads living a life on the move necessitated the capacity for them to be able to move camp from one location to another as circumstances

dictated and this is reflected in the ease with which they were able to pack up their temporary home and move. It is understood this operation could be completed within the daylight hours of the shortest day, facilitated mainly by the simplistic methods of disassembly and erection with materials specifically employed for the purpose and it is this distinct feature of nomadic life which differentiates them from the settled peoples. Modern-day nomads have the ability to dismantle the *ger*, pack up their entire building and load it onto a small truck within four hours, such is the level of sophistication associated with their prefabricated homes. The earliest form of prefabricated building, therefore, had its origins in architecture on the hoof but in more current times it is from the rear of a small truck, where flexibility and portability, together with ease of assembly, remain and form the prerequisites for the chosen lifestyle.

For the UK, history directs us to the earliest contribution of formalized prefabrication to the period of Britain's colonization when, in the mid-sixteenth and seventeenth centuries, the impetus to establish settlements was uppermost in locations like Australia, New Zealand, North America, India and so on. R.E. Smith (2010) refers to timber-framed components for housing being manufactured in Britain and shipped to various locations. It would be reasonable to suggest that for the users of the early nomadic tent or the

Mongolian *ger* under assembly.

British settlers' timber-panelled house, their relationship with the new environment within which they were sited was not identified in the context of architectural principles or planning rules but more for the structure to perform the function for which it was intended.

Manning's Portable Cottage

John Manning, a London carpenter and builder, had a clear and simple vision for providing immediate accommodation for his son landing in Australia in 1830. He was perhaps the pioneer in prefabrication as we might identify with today, although this was not obvious to the building industry at the time. Later known as the Manning Portable Colonial Cottage for Emigrants, the house was an expert system of prefabricated timber frame and infill components (Smith, R.E., 2010).

Simple timber panels were easily assembled within his workshop and, when secured together, provided the means with which to create a basic building structure and enclosure in one exercise. Here the wall panels were employed to perform the structure as well as the infill, very much akin to the conventional practice with masonry structure, except that for Manning the

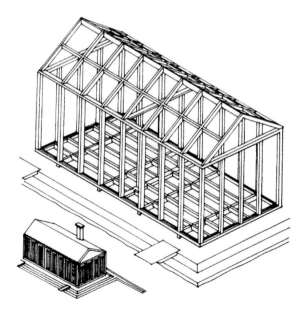

Manning's Portable Colonial Cottage for Emigrants.

structural wall panels were manufactured off-site and transported to the site (the colonies) for assembly. This very simple concept, synonymous with the principles of mass production, is representative of the first step into standardization and prefabrication practice. It paved the way for many more developments of standardization and prefabrication, not only in timber but also in concrete and steel later. For the ever-expanding British Empire of the 1800s which promoted settler expansion to the far reaches of its colonies, the concept of standardized prefabricated components was vital. It allowed for wall and roof panels to be shipped with the new settlers, thereby providing an instant housing solution without depending on the local natural environment for their building materials and supplies which, in some locations, might not even have existed. In many respects the concept is not too dissimilar to present-day practice where timber panels as a panelized or volumetric system are produced within a factory environment and transported to the site location where panels are incorporated into a conventional building process, or where modular units are assembled to create a modular building and, in some instances, shipped overseas but in the opposite direction to the transactions of the 1800s.

The concept that lies behind full standardization and prefabrication, epitomized by Manning's cottage design, was not really understood or exploited with the advances of the Industrial Revolution. Indeed, the manufacturing industrialist had more of a focus on an opportunity to manufacture 'parts' for a building at worst and 'building systems' at best. The thrust that lay behind the very early development of prefabrication was left mostly to the industrialist who naturally focused on producing buildings in the most cost-effective manner. Due to the absence of specific or meaningful architectural design expertise at the critical stage of its development, standardized prefabrication became a much despised approach within the built environment, as many of its effects are recalled by those of the Eastern Bloc countries in Europe and in the UK also. Manufacturing industrialists, however, were certainly alert to the opportunities and occupied the design void to best accommodate their investment on their own terms. The modularity that evolved at that time was more, by default, led by construction systems and assembly techniques originating from within the factory environment as opposed to being driven by architectural design. Consequently, solving the social problems of that time was led by building/construction applications, as opposed to architectural design solutions, where social need formed the principal ingredient as opposed to a desire for aesthetic quality. Architects and designers failed somewhat to recognize the potential of joining up architectural design with manufacturing and assembly processes.

Whilst the UK was already exporting prefabricated 'flat-pack' houses to the colonies around the 1800s the epitome of construction systems and prefabrication arrived in a more formal sense with the advent of the Industrial Revolution. This let loose a myriad of building systems and concepts surrounding standardization based on disciplined geometry where new manufacturing processes introduced standardized iron components. Standardization and prefabrication technology continued to be explored as a means for enhancing construction practice, but insufficient design expertise was employed (and by architects especially) to render the enterprise more viable aesthetically. Joseph Paxton, more a gardener than an architect, was instrumental in introducing some fresh design principles and particularly in relation to prefabrication. He identified a perfect solution whereby he satisfied his design brief by fulfilling a building's commercial obligations in parallel with delivering aesthetically as a natural process.

From Hand-Built to Factory-Made

Here we use 'construction' as being the construction processes relating to the built environment (the built environment being the entity for architecture) as opposed to construction processes that might apply to the building of aircraft, motor cars, telephone apparatus or similar complex items.

In order to understand what is meant by conventional forms of construction we need to appreciate firstly the characteristics that make up its ingredients. The term 'traditional' would suggest a method of construction employed over many generations which has become the conventional technique for construction dictated essentially by global location and materials available within that given place. For instance, a stone cottage in Wales is synonymous with this environment due to the abundance of natural stone that is easily quarried, just as a timber log cabin relates to the surroundings found in certain parts of America or within the Scandinavian countries, for example. Indeed, there remain numerous examples of traditional timber houses in the city of Vilnius in Lithuania where these historic buildings are still inhabited but nonetheless are located on the very edge of the commercial centre's more modern architecture.

Joseph Paxton's Crystal Palace for the Great Exhibition of 1851 highlights an early transition from the more hand-built construction practice to components manufactured in a factory and dispatched to the site for assembly. The Crystal Palace also highlighted a direction in prefabrication as the design brief set by the Building Committee, which included renowned engineers such as Isambard Kingdom Brunel and Robert Stephenson, who specified particular design requirements for a building to demonstrate to the world the status of British industry. By 15 March 1850 designers were invited to prepare and submit their design proposals. Fundamental to their submissions was that their designs had to deliver a building that must be temporary and that it had to be as simple and as economical as possible. Additionally, the building had to be economical to build and completed within the shortest possible time available prior to the grand opening scheduled for 1 May 1851. Architects submitting their designs for this competition were perhaps generally content to follow the aspirations and objectives of their existing aristocratic patrons and clients, but by 1850 Britain was in a new place socially and commercially.

Paxton showed interest in the project following the Building Committee's rejection of all 245 initial entries.

His design represented an excellent interpretation of prefabricated architecture and satisfied the design brief wherein the 10in × 49in size of the glass panes was dictated by the ability of the glass supplier. The cast-iron columns and girders, too, were manufactured within a factory and brought to the site for installation. Paxton's design demonstrated a clarity in standardization and modularity where the structural iron grid functioned in harmony with the capacity of the glass panels. Paxton's prefabricated Crystal Palace, then, is a purist vision of prefabricated architecture where factory manufacturing and assembly processes followed a design concept for the building in a purposeful and meaningful manner representing a beauty in its own right.

The dual concept of prefabrication and standardization expresses the attributes of the Industrial Revolution but not all of this form of enterprise provided the built environment with the most satisfactory design aesthetic. Expressions like 'unitized building' and 'building with systems' did not always convey a positive association with prefabrication and standardization. Indeed, there is evidence which prevails in the countless examples of prefabricated slab constructions within Eastern Europe (Staib et al., 2008) which provides credible reason for prefabricated architecture to be a totally bespoke design specialism only and for prefabrication to do its own thing under the auspices of manufacturing or as an aspect of the construction process (Knapp, 2013).

Prefabrication is not new; it has been with us for many centuries in one form or another, either totally made or aided to some degree through manufacturing and assembly processes. Within the last twenty years, especially with a leap forward in technology and manufacturing possibilities, prefabrication has presented itself as a viable alternative to conventional building methodologies. It is sometimes seen as a panacea for delivering buildings which might not otherwise be possible through conventional practices where the focus is on more building for less cost. Where negative perceptions surrounding prefabrication continue to exist in the current context, they tend to have remained as a mindset resulting from examples of poor design or poor construction or both. This is supported perhaps by the lack of any meaningful evidence to demonstrate that architects were engaged in the early manufacturing processes as part of the architectural design process. A common topic surrounding the prefabrication architecture debate is the absence of commitment from procurement officials to large-volume projects in order to make it sensible and financially viable for off-site manufacturers to engage totally and for architects to adopt a committed holistic approach to design where manufacturing and assembly process are integral to the building's prefabricated architectural design solution. Joseph Paxton, the gardener, was able to demonstrate over one hundred and fifty years ago a philosophy of simplicity applied to prefabricated architecture; standardization in its purest form has since been taken through numerous iterations of development but not necessarily with laudable distinction in terms of prefabricated architecture being a credible entity in design expertise.

Industrial Design within the Built Environment

Prefabrication is a vast topic covering many aspects of modern living and existence. It embraces a number of sectors and design disciplines, and impacts no less on any one facet due to the natural interaction of them all. Within the scope of prefabrication, however, the built environment is perhaps one entity where it has demonstrated a marked influence and accounts for many unfavourable perceptions held within the UK. The built environment represents the epitome of all our respective cultures by demonstrating the nature and extent of our technological skills, construction techniques and design capabilities. For centuries we applied these skills and techniques to create our housing, schools and hospitals under the umbrella of low-rise or community architecture. As the commercial environments evolved, we created business and financial centres and parks to depict such enterprise, albeit consisting of medium to high-rise buildings. Within the specific discipline of prefabricated architecture then, where technology and evolving construction techniques compete with architecture as a disciplined art, there remains a preference by some to distinguish building as a science and architecture as an art. Moreover, the separation and disconnect which continues to prevail highlights all the more the lack of real commitment of government departments to embrace this new science of building and for architects to embrace manufacturing and assembly as a new art in architecture.

Buildings and their construction techniques remain a constant activity and process in the formation of the built environment since humankind first considered ways and means of providing itself with basic shelter. The various building alternatives employed throughout the ages have varied immensely, as indeed have the array of structural systems adopted, dictated largely by location, climate and the availability of local materials for the building project. Early examples of construction systems highlighted the desire for flexibility, quick easy assembly and dismantling with efficiency, given the nomadic nature of earlier man. The urgency surrounding cost-effectiveness coupled with aspects associated with environmental context and fit only presented themselves as issues much later in the evolution of humans' awareness of their natural and built environment where a greater focus perhaps lay eventually within settlements. Current demands on the construction process in relation to delivering buildings within a built environment are perhaps more challenging as the quest for more efficient and cost-effective building solutions remains ever-present. In the UK prefabricated housing has dominated a debate since 'prefabs' were introduced by the Ministry of Works as a means to overcome the housing shortage following World War Two; negative perceptions which remain ingrained within many have produced a mindset which appears to continue through the generations within the UK.

Terms of Reference

The term 'built environment' refers to surroundings shaped by humankind, either by design or default, for the purpose of its own activity and interaction, whether for living, working or recreation. The built environment varies in scale from one's own personal space to large industrial spaces that may be shared in the performance of a function. The built environment is shaped by the scale of those spaces that are formed by structures referred to as buildings (sometimes architectural gems) and they come in all shapes and sizes, from humans' first shelters to single buildings and groups of building enclosures, in a considered fashion, and eventually to neighbourhoods and cities. The context for our environment at any one time is, in the first instance, dictated by the total building structures, and secondly by the materials and components employed in their assembly, all of which express an architectural composition. Technology, building materials (whether local or imported), construction processes available in any given location, climate, local culture and context will all add to the mix in producing the form of the built environment, by which the very soul of the place is identified generally and especially by those in occupation. These ingredients, which stand behind every new building project, are depicted by their construction, building processes and methodologies. They are in turn further influenced (and enhanced hopefully) by advancing technology and expertise and a measure of purposeful design where architectural literacy prevails.

The human mind can and is expected to absorb many things at one time. The degree to which this function will happen with any measure of efficiency and accuracy is dictated in many respects by the environment within which humankind finds itself. Our environment, whether natural or built, is composed of various elements and scales. Our built environment, being made up of buildings or groups of buildings and structures, forms an immediate reference to our subconscious and our appreciation of the aesthetic represents what we see. The relationship of human scale to that of our environment will act as a major catalyst for the way in which we respond to it. Out of necessity, during some point in our lives, we might find ourselves removed from our own individual

Single-storey and multi-storey buildings defining human scale within a built environment.

environment where the scale of that local vernacular represents all that is precious to us. That is not to suggest, however, that an alternative (whether it consists of the wilds of open exposed countryside or the soul of an inner city) is incorrect as the reliance on our own individual perception of environment will dictate our response to it, whether it is good or bad. The common denominator in all environments is scale and it is to scale that the human mind will relate in the first instance.

Modernist architects of the early twentieth century appear not to have grasped this relationship. Their perception of modularity introduced scale as represented by the large panel of emptiness, devoid of human scale or relationships, as opposed to the modularity of the previous classical order. Whilst there is nothing inappropriate in producing large buildings as such, there is nonetheless discord when the primary elements of that building are of such sizes and dimension as to be so divorced from human meaning and empathy. The early modernist architect might be expected to have had a better understanding of the human scale and the subdivision of elements identified as fractals (Mandelbrot, 1975) as the previous generation of architectural design was founded on classical proportions. Fractal characteristics in architecture relate to a geometry which architects sometimes identify as a 'module' for organizing the primary architectural element (Joye, 2007), and this has particular relevance in relation to the modularity of the building's structural organization. Salingaros

and West (1999) refer to the visual balance within substructures and to varying scales provided by the elements displayed within. Composition is derived from a basic mathematical rule on the number and arrangement of sub-elements, which Mandelbrot refers to as fractals, contained within the main structure. Early twentieth-century architects proposed major stylistic changes without perhaps having a full appreciation at that time of how the human eye-to-brain system works. Now there is perhaps a better acceptance of the larger empty panel as architectural style has evolved, with present generations possessing an updated aesthetic, more by default maybe, having become more accustomed and familiar with greater sense of scale. We are perhaps more tolerant in accepting the large empty panel, albeit with minimum interruption necessitated by jointing or connections, as a representation of a clean uncluttered architectural graphic indicative of the minimalist aesthetic, although Salingaros and West (1999) may not agree.

Architecture is derived from a series of intellectual and physical activities where the design process is led by the architect. Whilst some within the project team may insist on influencing its direction in a particular way for specific reasons, usually cost, the architect's professional indemnity insurance is a useful tool for generating a sober response on issues surrounding change and adjustment to specification. Architecture is considered to be an art form and is differentiated from other art forms because of its ability to provide function. It is three-dimensional and it allows its internal

Large panels
with subdivision
of elements
deliver minimalist
architecture.

Private house
exterior showing
empty panel space.

and external spaces to be occupied usually for a specific purpose. Architecturally then, the use of standardized prefabricated elements and components to accelerate the provision of unitized housing during the twentieth century could be deemed as correct as it performed the function for which it was intended. The result of the prefabricated manufacturing process, therefore, is that which arrives on the site for installation. The ability to classify its aesthetic as a design in architectural language is challenging therefore, as its terms of reference are founded within a language of industrialization and manufacturing which adheres to a set of different rules. Architectural and aesthetic labels did not matter to the municipal authorities facing a chronic housing shortage, nor to the people seeking a place to live, nor indeed to the industrialist whose business it was to stay in business, and there is nothing new in that. The concept surrounding standardized manufactured unitized housing solutions based on prefabricated and modular options is not invalid for what it is intended for, and architecturally that is correct. What is absent, perhaps, is the connection to an aesthetic and a built environment which presents a visual relationship for human consumption. Paxton's Crystal Palace achieved much of what was desired. Not only did his understanding of architecture and aesthetic instil a new order in design by delivering a building for a specific purpose but, more significantly, a new design discipline which can only be identified as prefabricated and modular architecture: PAMA.

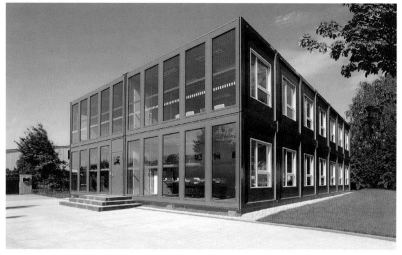

Modular building superstructure completed in factory to 90 per cent and now under final assembly at the site.

Modular office building completed in factory to 90 per cent and now completed.

Prefabrication and Design Freedom

Housing and Prefabrication

By the beginning of the twentieth century, Europe was struggling to cope with the massive housing shortage: this continued to the end of World War One and beyond. Given the magnitude of the social housing requirement it could not be satisfied by the traditional trades system as in previous generations. Industrialization was already well established where the large-scale production of goods and products was available at more economical rates, and manufacturing companies and industrialists were always ready to recognize new business opportunities. As purveyors of manufactured products, the industrialists' primary focus was naturally to produce a product to fit the immediate need and the chronic housing shortage was an ideal candidate. The ingredients for the manufacturing industrialist were perfect and, as a ready-made market evolved throughout most of Europe's cities, demand continued to expand, coupled with the potential for mass-produced manufacturing as a result. Not all manufacturing industrialists of the period may be identified for their prowess in architectural design but their agility to identify a business opportunity, married to their ability to make profitable products, was their speciality. By the outbreak of World War Two prefabrication had demonstrated itself to be a perfect fit as an evolving set of manufacturing processes in an era of extensive and expanding industrialization.

UNI-SECO

At the end of World War Two, some industrialists and manufacturers transitioned from manufacturing war armaments to manufacturing homes. Names such as SECO, Arcon, Tarran and AIROH became synonymous with manufacturing prefabricated homes throughout the UK.

SECO was conceived in 1940 when the UK government was faced with the problem of providing housing for the thousands of workers needed in the new factories. The company's directors identified then that the traditional methods of building would not be able to provide all the accommodation that was needed quickly enough. In their brochure produced during the war they describe their system as one comprised of wall units (unitized wall panels

Typical SECO prefab houses using panelized construction: Excalibur Estate, Catford, London. (Photo by author)

Road view of houses on Excalibur Estate, Catford, London. (Photo by author)

as assemblies) and components. Whilst seeking to respond to the urgent demand during the war they also demonstrated in their brochure a vision for the time after the hostilities. Reference is made to SECO's facilities specifically set up to provide training for their outside contractors, of which there were about two hundred companies, to train in their assembly process prior to actually executing a build on the site. There is no reference to 'construction' on-site, only assembly. Indeed, it is stated in their brochure that 'Prefabrication is a matter of degree. It means, simply stated, the factory production of composite building units for dry assembly of the building site'. Whilst the end product always resulted in a volumetric building, the putting together of the parts, components and assemblies was nonetheless an on-site construction process consisting of panel assemblies, components and parts as opposed to a three-dimensional volumetric unit.

Parts, Components and Aesthetics

Literature highlights the attributes and constraints of early prefabrication and the negative perceptions which continue to prevail even today. Some of these criticisms and negatively-held views are well justified and indeed are well founded, given that many of the early examples of prefabricated housing epitomize solely the essence of pure industrialized manufacture rather than any relationship to architectural articulation. Vale (1996) refers to Lethaby who, in 1911, suggested the aim should be to produce housing with the same degree of efficiency as manufacturing a bicycle (a prime example of standardization) in order to satisfy the housing shortage urgency. Similar comparisons by Le Corbusier and Gropius refer to a manufacturing ethos in relation to automobiles and aeroplanes which, in essence, are more orientated toward the mass production associated with the bicycle. Henry Ford in turn took mass production and standardization, under the guise of multiple units, to the next level in manufacturing processes.

The aesthetic form resulting from the manufacture of the early bicycle or the Ford motor car is founded on the materials and components used in the manufacturing process in conjunction with references to style for that time. Similarly, early prefabricated components and elements produced for housing did not necessarily adopt any particular architectural style or aesthetic but followed manufacturing processes first: its direction embraced a manufacturing simplicity which was often perceived later as bland, brutal and somewhat unforgiving for some occupiers and users. Prefabricated panels of concrete in early twentieth-century housing projects were born out of a similar manufacturing ethos with little, if any, architectural design expertise engagement from architects and seemingly little, if any, reference to surrounding environments. The fabrication sizes and proportions of panels were at best considered in manufacturing terms but largely bereft of any architectural design expertise or art in relation to the completed building. For much of the twentieth century the lack of continuity in architectural and urban design relating to the site context and the evolution of the built environment as a consequence remains a constant vision in the minds of many. With the absence of dedicated architectural representation at two vital stages, namely manufacturing processes and on-site construction/installation, early prefabricated housing in the form of low-, medium- and high-rise apartment blocks evolved into a dedicated industrialized design entity with engineering as the primary design discipline, appointed largely to ensure the structure remained in place.

Social housing project in London by Peabody Trust, completed in 2003 and delivered through modular building.

Early 1960s low-rise panelized construction with large prefabricated concrete panels.

It is difficult to see where architectural design freedom might flourish in a conventional sense within a manufacturing culture where industrial design became automatic and predicable, shrouded by urgency, suitability, speed and profit. Architects especially have to recognize the design opportunities and challenges they failed to embrace with regard to harnessing the prefabricated technology that prevailed. Rather than employ the art of design as part of their remit in contributing to society through the practice of their particular craft and design specialism, they opted to remove themselves from the manufacturing arena. Corbusier, too, had a struggle in reconciling architectural beauty deriving from industrialization when his terms of reference were allied more to ancient Greek architecture. Architects in Europe generally could be accused of standing aloof from the evolving science and technology associated with standardized prefabrication whilst architects in America, on the other hand, it is suggested, committed more readily to the concept of designing for prefabrication. Goodman (2017) highlights the affinity American architects had with prefabrication and cites the work of A. Lawrence Kocher who, when editor of the *Architectural Record* (1927–38), introduced 'prefabrication and standardized detailing

to the American architectural profession'. Kocher possessed different social awareness from 'that of his European social democratic contemporaries' but, even for Goodman, this level of commitment to prefabrication technology was deemed to be somewhat minimum, given its significance and potential impact in terms of producing housing for all.

The willingness of the industrialist to respond to the housing shortage in a meaningful way, uninhibited by design philosophies normally held by architects, is evidenced by the examples on display through Europe for most of the twentieth century. Ingredients such as these will always outweigh design principles employed by architects in previous centuries which Knapp (2013) refers to as periods of 'intellectual retrenchment architecture'. However, being so wedded to a previous era they not only lost sight of their responsibility to society as architects but missed out completely on a new and evolving design discipline in prefabricated architecture. Architects also isolated themselves from lucrative business opportunities, where overall control of the total design and manufacturing prefabrication enterprise was within their grasp. For now mass production remains the forte of the industrial engineer – so let them maintain claim over that territory as bespoke architectural design is the true speciality of the architect (Knapp, 2013).

The Changing Nature and Extent of Prefabrication

Introduction

Whilst prefabrication continues to evolve, driven in no small measure by the housing shortages that have existed since the early twentieth century, innovation in design and technology evolves in parallel. Since the last economic downturn in 2008, which in some respects continues in the UK in relation to community architecture and architect involvement, the urgency to deliver buildings more quickly with greater cost-efficiencies remains omnipresent. No longer is the sole focus on housing, chronic though it is: other sectors too, such as schools and universities, hospitals, health and social care, libraries, sports and recreational buildings and the like, all present themselves as worthy contenders.

Over the past twenty years some degree of innovation and advances in technology have succeeded in reducing the negative perceptions associated with prefabrication and OSM generally. However, a continuing reluctance to exploit these technical advances appears to be met with a lack of collaboration, enthusiasm or vision, or all three, among clients, architects and contractors as a preference to function within the current status quo continues to prevail. For the construction industry to have a worthwhile future it needs to examine the advances surrounding artificial intelligence, machine automation and the technologies embracing 3D printing and seek to identify the most suitable aspects for taking the UK into the twenty-first century prefabrication technology. The alternative to the conventional build practice already exists in UK OSM where industrialists recognize the business opportunities. Albeit these are restricted somewhat at present for most manufacturers undertaking large-scale high-rise projects, but this will not last forever, as the Croydon UK modular project demonstrates.

Core Elements Defining Prefabrication

Consider for a moment an assembly system which relates to the world and scale of many young people, and some adults too, where the notions of prefabrication, standardization and components are viewed in very simple terms. Take a world-famous name such as Lego; this is synonymous with creative minds running riot with building objects, modelling buildings and creating spaces and environments based on simple plastic modular bricks that lock together. The evolution of Lego – from a carpentry joinery business through one making wooden toys, on to their famous modular plastic brick and ultimately to assembly systems which incorporate interconnecting plastic rods, wheels and individual parts of numerous descriptions – demonstrates a simplistic understanding of the prefabrication and modularization concept. Entirely based on a similar modularity and connectivity, it remains a well-tested utilization of components that are manufactured to a prescribed specification, incorporating standardization and precision as the primary focus of the assembly process. The components and sub-assemblies come together with ease and confidence based on precision and exactness where it is known from the outset what the final result is expected to be. A simple toy model assemblage that embraces a standardized modularity begins with a raw material that results in a collection of familiar plastic modular components and individual parts which Ung (2018) describes as the three tiers of prefabrication. The components, when gathered together and placed in a box, occupy the minimum of space and are delivered to the customer as a self-assembly entity. The contents constitute all that is required to self-build the model fire station, the police station, the extravagant castle or urban scene which can be repeated many times over, and often is. The box of components for specific Lego

Basic Lego modular interconnecting bricks.

Urban scene created entirely with Lego's system of standardized modular components.

Installation of new modular facility for urban training at Camp Taji, Iraq, June 2019.

Whether prefabrication is applied to a very simple Lego-scale project as described above or to a multimillion-pound building project involving prefabricated and modular components at a number of different levels and complexity, the design principles and manufacturing processes involved are, in the main, very similar. The more complex the building project, however, the more demanding the various levels of management and coordination are for the client. 'A building project, regardless of its production method, is an ambitious undertaking. The sheer number of individuals, teams, materials, products, systems, communication, and finances that are implicit in the finished building is difficult to fathom' (Smith, 2010, p. 80). Irrespective of how the building project is to be procured from the factory process, as opposed projects, of which there are many, is designed to be an economic and efficient solution for manufacturing purposes with minimum wasted materials but, especially, designed to be very simple for the young creator or builder to assemble a project within the minimum amount of time.

to being hand-built conventionally on the site, complexities and challenges are always present. That said, substituting the conventional route for prefabrication with manufacturing and assembly processes presents its own specific skill requirements where the unique expertise and experience of professionals is called for, especially in relation to project decisions and coordination.

There are a number of core elements that distinguish prefabrication and premanufacture as specific disciplines. Prefabrication represents the manufacture of components and parts used in the execution of conventional build projects where OSM constitutes a part, predominantly in relation to the superstructure. Premanufacture, on the other hand, surrounds the entire process of manufacturing modular units or modules that are assembled together at the site location. Prefabrication is a generic term applied in a number of ways, discussed under different topics and terminologies. In more recent years a measure of confusion has evolved as a consequence. Inconsistency surrounding the actual identity of component prefabrication or premanufactured modular units when applied to panelization and modularization continues to prevail, not only in the mind of the layperson, but sometimes in the minds of practitioners and professionals who operate within the industry. The term 'prefabrication' is used in so many different ways with different meanings and understandings that its clarity of purpose and focus for effective integration has been lost (Knapp, 2013). R.E. Smith (2010) cites the contemporary Merriam-Webster's Dictionary in order to provide a workable meaning of the word 'prefabrication'. The dictionary states that 'prefabrication' means to 'fabricate the parts at a factory so that construction consists mainly of assembling and uniting standardized parts'. The House of Lords Report (2017–19), on the other hand, refers to off-site manufacture as 'an example of modern methods of construction' where the connotation relates to factory activities, or cites it as 'an umbrella term encompassing many different systems'; Kier Construction in their submission to the Report suggest off-site manufacture as 'the design,

planning, manufacture and pre-assembly of construction elements or components in a factory environment prior to installation-site at their intended, final location'. Written evidence presented by Accord Housing Association for the same House of Lords Report highlights 'confusion in terms of terminology'. In further written evidence a London-based architect lays claim to the term 'modular building' for a housing project under way in June 2000 where modular building techniques are cited. The word 'techniques' was a familiar expression used in the past when seeking to describe construction activities which had a factory input. It did not lay claim to any specific or clear identity or focus (Knapp, 2013) in relation to describing panelized construction as a method of construction or premanufactured modular buildings as a totally factory process. Neither was the construction industry nor the manufacturing fraternity clear as to how best to classify evolving techniques except to suggest elements of the on-site construction activities being moved to the factory as a prefabrication process of some sorts, supposedly in the name of efficiency and cost-effectiveness. In all of these scenarios the factory environment and not the construction site forms the nucleus of current thinking in relation to prefabrication, irrespective of whether a panelized construction or a premanufactured modular building is the result.

There are various titles and nametags employed within the construction industry which have a relevance to prefabrication to a certain degree, but which may not depict specific aspects of prefabricated and modular architecture accurately. Currently, 'prefabrication' is a term often used to describe aspects of conventional construction. In other words, where certain elements, parts or components derive from a factory manufacturing process they are in essence prefabricated as they are produced away from the construction site; this is currently identified as 'off-site manufacturing' (OSM).

To illustrate this, prefabrication/OSM for some is identified as modular; to others it is merely part of an existing construction process irrespective of its manufacturing, on-site installation or site assembly methodologies. 'Unitized building' differs from 'system building' just as 'modular construction' competes with 'modular buildings' for precise identification. Panelized construction favours differently from volumetric modular design by the very manner in which the prefabricated entity contributes to the actual process on the site. All of these, and more besides, have one common denominator – prefabrication, and for some professional practitioners and clients alike, is described as 'OSM' or 'modern methods of construction' (MMC) as an overarching all-embracing identity. Bourke et al. (2007, p. 284) refer to MMC as '... a broad range of construction types ranging from complete housing systems built in factories through to new site-based technologies.' Within the mix of modern methods of construction then, prefabrication can be defined as a means by which the raw materials as individual parts are manufactured in a particular manner or process to produce a completed prefabricated component. These components in turn are used to create modular units, sometimes referred to as volumetric units or modules, which have a three-dimensional entity. Components, too, are manufactured as modularized panels and dispatched to the site for installation as part of the conventional construction process on-site.

Where the word 'prefabricate' is employed as a transitive verb, the corresponding noun, 'prefabrication', demonstrates parts that are produced within a pure manufacturing environment and then delivered to the site location for installation or final assembly. So, where does the 'pre' in 'prefabrication' derive from? The answer is not difficult to find when reminded of the traditional hand-building practices and skills of the site that are being transferred to and substituted by manufacturing and assembly process within the factory. Buildings consisting of prefabricated parts and components that are assembled into modular units within the factory and delivered to the site for final assembly ultimately generate the completed assemblage, resulting in a modular building. In this sense, the expression 'modular building' is used as a

noun as opposed to the transitive verb where 'modular building' or 'construction' depicts a conventional building or construction process on the site and not a factory process. It is also worth noting that the final assembling of volumetric modular units at the site is predominantly a function completed by the manufacturer as the final phase of his assembly process and not by the main contractor who is engaged only in on-site conventional construction. Similarly, panelization is represented by panel systems more often installed by the panel manufacturer as a means of contributing to conventional construction projects. The installation of the panels is a separate work package and does not accomplish a completely finished building in the way a premanufactured modular building does.

Prefabrication

The primary elements which constitute prefabrication are therefore panelization and modularization. They are both identified as being derived from a factory manufacturing process and a clear distinction exists between the two by the different manner in which the two entities contribute to the procurement process, jointly and individually. It would be naive to believe that panelized and modularized building have the capacity to provide absolute and total automatic cure-all building solutions offering entirety in terms of cost-effectiveness, time-efficiencies, health and safety benefits, sustainability, speed of erection, improved delivery processes and the like, as this is clearly not the case. There are, of course, numerous prefabrication alternatives and options for the clients to procure buildings and the attributes and constraints associated with the same comprise an area of specialist knowledge and expertise that clients would be well advised to refer to.

In essence, 'prefabrication' is a global term applied to both panelization (*see* Chapter 5) and modular buildings (not construction) (as discussed here and in Chapter 6), where panelization is an on-site construction method and modular buildings result from premanufacturing and assembly processes within a factory. Whenever 'modular building' is referred to there is an inference which suggests all things have a modular connotation but without any distinction as to which elements of the superstructure are modularized or even panelized. Inaccurate differentiation occurs when the panelized components, such as wall panels and floors and roof cassettes, are used to substitute for conventional materials for a building, and the distinction as to whether the building is conventionally built or modular built is the dilemma. In fact, with panelization there is no building modularity or modular buildings resulting in this instance as no modular units have been premanufactured.

Panelized Construction

Panelization embraces all aspects associated with OSM, ranging from fabricating panels to creating walls and cassettes to forming floors and roofs. Panelization, then, could be identified as a 'kit of parts', or 'flat-pack' in some instances, where panelized walls, floors and roofs are manufactured specifically for a building which is designed to take advantage of the attributes associated with this specific manufacturing process. It is closely associated with on-site construction as it forms part of the conventional construction

process, given that its installation is an on-site activity. Prefabricated panelized walls, floors and roof sections can also be of a specialist nature and in such situations they come under the auspices of a specialist sub-contractor's work package in the normal way for a conventional construction project. (*See* the section 'Open and Closed Panel Options' in Chapter 5.)

Modular Buildings

Modular buildings are significantly different from panelized buildings in that they constitute a complete entity, an end product that is premanufactured and delivered for final assembly at the site location. The size of the intended building dictates the number of modular units required.

As all of the premanufacturing, assembly and fitting out is completed within the factory there is no 'construction' of the sort normally associated with conventional on-site activities, merely final assembly of the modular units at the site location. Terminology used for identifying a modular building therefore does not include 'modular construction' and the distinction between modular construction and 'a modular building' is already made (*see* Chapters 5 and 6). Modular

Single modular unit consisting of a hotel bedroom on each side of a central corridor. Manufacturer as principal contractor for the client coordinates all project design, factory assembly and complete fitting out of modular units with delivery and on-site assembly. (Courtesy of CIMC-MBS Ltd)

building is a factory manufacturing process producing standardized modules in volumetric formats both large and small; the largest module size is governed by the size of a delivery vehicle's route to the site and then accessing the location of the works on the site. The management and control of the assembly process is dictated by whether the project is being delivered to the client through a conventional procurement route (that is, via a main contractor) or direct from the manufacturer. Delivering a modular building consisting of one or a number (large or small) of volumetric units can be provided totally by an off-site manufacturer and does not necessarily require the involvement of a main contractor in the conventional sense.

In all of the above references what is particularly regretful is the total absence of any meaningful reference to design and especially in an architectural context. It is not sufficient to consider prefabrication and off-site manufacture solely in relation to aspects surrounding construction only. It is certainly much more than that. Prefabrication as a set of factory processes is a holistic enterprise where architectural design at concept stage should embrace all aspects associated with the fabrication design, manufacturing and assembly processes within the factory through to how the on-site panel installation or modular assemblage is catered for within the overall design process. Prefabricated and modular architecture, therefore, is quite distinct from off-site manufacture and modern methods of construction as such, because PAMA occupies a manufacturing process commencing with the architect's design concept and completing with the finished building at the site.

Allied to PAMA is another significant feature which epitomises the very essence of the prefabrication concept – and that is *standardization*.

Standardization and System Building

Standardization

In the early years of the twentieth century industrialists recognized a business opportunity with regard to satisfying a market demand. Housing shortages at that time were responded to not by architects but mainly by manufacturers promoting system building solutions consisting of everything from pre-cast concrete to steel frame and timber frame. Essentially, the most attractive feature for the manufacturer was standardization, with wall, floor and roof panels manufactured identically and repeated for the same building solution many times over. Unitization was born. It is difficult to identify an architecture resulting from a manufactured process of this nature except to recognize and accept the end result as its own architecture for what it is. Unitized and standardized building systems might account for a less than favourable impression of prefabrication as polite architecture fails to be represented.

A distinction between vernacular and polite architecture is made where the vernacular is a representation of building with no input from a trained professional, relying more on the local knowledge, market demands, materials and customs of indigenous inhabitants from a particular region. As with the Mongolian nomads the essence of vernacular architecture, then, is associated more with the amateur designer whose primary focus is applied more to the functionality of the building for a given local environmental context and less so to any reference to a design order or international style (Brunskill, 2000). Brunskill identifies the input of a trained professional architect to a design objective as being the ultimate in polite architecture where reference is drawn from an 'international fashion, style or set of conventions' and where the aesthetic rather than the functional demands.

The nature and extent of standardization achieved as the primary entity in a building's design will dictate the viability of the manufacturing process and the materials used. The industrialist and manufacturer have always had a natural affinity with standardization. It is innate and instinctive for them to know how to mass-produce their products in the most efficient and cost-effective manner for them to be commercially viable, if not immediately, then certainly over a short period of time if the business is to survive. Historically and even today, little if any appreciation appears to be present for architectural design philosophies, articulation, intellect and the like surrounding standardized or customized prefabrication. Fabrication considerations and preferences often hijack architectural design, resulting in an end product where stylized displays are delivered at best with a focus only on the two-dimensional visual, and even then this can be at a superficial level mostly.

Traditional Practice

Historically, within the construction site environment the initial fabricated elements were predominantly carried out on-site. In other words, prior to the introduction of industrialization which instigated off-site prefabrication in the first instance, the actual construction of buildings depended solely upon the on-site assembly of raw materials such as timber, bricks, stone and so on, and upon the skill of the tradespeople to achieve the completed building. In other words, buildings were hand-built on the construction site. When industrialization arrived in earnest, followed by the advanced levels of technology that exist at present, the various sections or elements of the building being put together or fabricated away from the site environment can be deemed to be 'prefabricated'. A vast body of the work normally associated with site activities was superseded by the ability to prefabricate the same where time, cost and quality control evolved as principal features of the process and which remain today with an even greater urgency and expectancy. 'Off-site manufacturing' (OSM) is a common term used to differentiate between that which happens on the site and that which takes place within a factory environment but very often used without fully appreciating precisely the nature and extent of the separation or overlapping of activities.

A school of thought prevails among some off-site manufacturers seeking to capitalize on the current growing urgency that the objective is merely to deliver buildings ever more quickly and cheaply. It is believed by some that their function is to relocate as much of the on-site activity as possible to within a factory environment. This would suggest, therefore, that a licence exists for the factory to operate to the same tolerances expected within the on-site environment. This is clearly not the case and in many respects is responsible for the continued negative impression attributed to factory production and site installation in some instances. Current practice indicates the determination to win the project is not matched by the ability of some manufacturers to deliver a finished product which equates to expectations. Neither is it matched by the level of precision deemed necessary if anxieties and perceptions over quality and robustness are to be alleviated. In order for OSM processes to have any credibility the ethos surrounding prefabrication design and production specialisms must adhere to more exacting standards.

For PAMA to announce its presence and become relevant it will require significant input from the trained architect who is prepared to adopt standardization and manufacturing processes as an intrinsic element of the design process. It is the trained architect who must take the lead in all aspects of design where manufacturing and assembly are integral to his or her overall architectural solution, irrespective of whether the concept design embraces standardization, bespoke design or a combination of both. For architects, the correlation between designing to the rules of standardized geometry associated with modularity against that of a 'free plan' design (bespoke design) are never too dissimilar as the 'module' has been a standard means of measurement for centuries starting with the ancient Greeks: their most ideal exponent of modular design can be identified within their temples. Until more recently, however, there has been a greater emphasis for architects to maintain a sense, (but a sense only) of the 'free plan' design approach in spite of being obliged to introduce a degree of modularity through structural necessity and sensible economics (the structural grid). This may not be referred to as 'modular' construction by architectural purists but the introduction of a structural grid does by default embrace the essence of modularity insofar as ordered geometry is evident. Consequently, it would be architecturally naive to suggest the majority of building projects are without any modularity at all, especially where cost- and time-efficiencies are a prerequisite and usually adhered to. It follows, therefore, that PAMA already prevails, under the guise of manufacturing and assembly through the off-site manufacturer, but the missing ingredient so far, however, is the absence of the trained architect.

Over the past twenty years prefabrication has enjoyed a small renaissance, with the benefit of new technology and automation, the application of new materials and new on-site installation and assembly process married to a capacity for quality design not previously applied to prefabricated architecture as a design discipline. Regretfully, among architects and construction professionals, prefabricated building continues to adopt a culture of separation where architectural design does not form any part of the manufacturing process. Overcoming this disconnect is integral to the future success and acceptance of PAMA as a design discipline where the trained architect leads at the front end of the process.

Manufacture and Assembly Technology

Over periods of history we have benefited from the great architectural styles reflecting the opulence and grandeur that prevailed at certain times. From the ancient Celts to the Egyptians to the Greeks and then the Romans up to the eighteenth and nineteenth centuries, architecture has depicted more significant examples of humankind's greatness to itself. Constructing buildings today in many respects reflects the same essential ingredients that have existed throughout the ages, albeit with a lesser degree of opulence perhaps, but with a far greater focus on cost-efficiencies and functionality. In essence, buildings have always consisted of walls, floors and roofs together with a myriad of mechanical and electrical services to varying degrees and, whilst the reason for creating different types of buildings has evolved through the necessity of functionality, they nonetheless serve the purposes for humankind.

With the various styles of architecture came the various methods of construction and none more significant than the introduction of quick assembly processes made possible by the Industrial Revolution of the mid-nineteenth century in Britain and its influences throughout its empire. Naturally, technology has moved on and to a point where, within current trends and expectations, buildings can be constructed through numerous techniques with varying materials and high technological design in order to achieve the ultimate cost-efficient building. Design aspects relating to the application of the technology, then, form a partnership which demonstrates a key ingredient within the completed structure, referred to as the architecture and its aesthetic.

Irrespective of the type of building under consideration, whether housing, commercial or health and recreational buildings, they are all strongly influenced by technology. Johnson and Giorgis (2002) affirm the influence technology has on the design of buildings within which architecture and its aesthetic reside. Extending this theory for architectural design generally will naturally include prefabrication as part of the design process. Moreover, where the architectural design is integral to the manufacturing and assembly process from the outset as a joined-up enterprise, it offers a total representation of architectural design and manufacturing in harmony under the auspices of prefabricated and modular architecture.

Precision a Prerequisite

In order for architects to pay more serious attention to what manufacturing has to offer in terms of design options, it must demonstrate the ability to provide a precision product from beginning to end. Many architects in the UK do not have a concentration of work in high volumes. Indeed, many of the projects can be small infill sites or single one-off residential projects, small school projects or additions to sports clubs or sports halls perhaps, all of which are ideal projects to be designed, manufactured and delivered as prefabricated solutions. Within the UK the size of many of the manufacturing companies is reflected accordingly. Many may not be properly geared up with precision machinery or wall-to-wall automation to respond to the quality and precision expectations being demanded. Whilst not commonplace within the UK perhaps, technology and automated machinery already exist to respond to the small-scale projects where precision and exactness are the norm, where productivity is significantly increased too and within a smaller (under 325m²/3,500ft²) space requirement. Even within the larger UK manufacturing companies the concept of PAMA does not fully accord with expectations of architects for precision and exactness. More significant, perhaps, is the urgency for architects to adopt manufacturing and assembly technology as integral to their concept design process. For now, the section of the manufacturing industry seeking to accommodate the building industry

Factory automation delivering effective production from a smaller-size factory. (Courtesy of Frame Homes (SW) Ltd)

tends to be populated by the larger operators who are attracted to high-volume manufacturing projects in the main. Large-volume projects tend not to be forthcoming for many reasons, as cited in the House of Lords Report (2017–19), of which precision and exactness is a feature of the enquiry.

Behind the completed building, however, lies some very ingenious machine technology, especially where a measure of architectural design input accompanies the fabrication process as a joined-up operation. Prefabricated building solutions consist of many options, from a simple jointing system that allows materials and components to be connected in a very efficient way to the total processes involved in manufacturing complete walls with all doors and windows incorporated within the complete assembled panelized modular component. Indeed, with the totally factory-assembled modular component installed on-site or completed modular units assembled on-site one could suggest the building's architecture is designed to be built by way of the prefabricated modular component or the three-dimensional module.

Prefabrication and modular architecture by and large revolve around its technology, the emerging automation, artificial intelligence and the manner in which the raw materials are converted from materials into components and complete assemblies that fit into the manufacturing and assembly process for on-site installation or final assembly. The more simplistic the technology employed in the prefabrication process for a given component to a modular unit, the more likely it is that prefabricated architecture will result. Moreover, the architect might declare that architecture and design quality derive from simplicity; the constructor or client on the other hand will maintain the beauty of the completed building lies within the ease of construction and the cost-efficient result, namely profit. Given the myths that surround prefabricated architecture, certain features and specific issues such as delivery dates, cost-efficiencies and suitability tend to be uppermost in the minds of the decision-makers and less so perhaps on the niceties of architectural design. Therein lies the challenge for the architect more than the manufacturer.

Chapter Two

Perceptions and Current Influences

Prefabrication and Perception

Introduction

Historically it has been perceived that prefabrication does not lend itself to architecture but this is not accurate. This would be to suggest that the architect is incapable of designing buildings through the medium of prefabricated manufacture and system design. Prefabrication in building has existed now for over one hundred and fifty years and has passed through a myriad of architectural styles and fashions during this time. Whilst the design expertise of the trained architect may not have been apparent for much of this time, there remains notwithstanding a culture in prefabrication which for some holds treasured nostalgic memories although for others less flattering descriptions are often involved.

Whilst prefabrication established a presence in the twentieth century in an endeavour to solve the massive housing crisis in Europe, it brought with it a move away from traditional construction techniques (hand-built technology) to that where machine technology became its nucleus. Clearly, the timber or asbestos sheet-clad 'hut' solution within the UK was conceived as a temporary one only and built accordingly to fulfil that purpose. In this regard it performed its function and in many instances performed it very well, not because it was an instant and economic build solution (because it was), nor because the architectural aesthetic was a design feature of any intrinsic value (because it wasn't), but the overall product has stood the test of time and in many instances has outlived its life expectancy.

It is well documented that perceptions surrounding prefabrication in the UK have historically been

Prefabricated building style circa 1945.

Perceptions of prefabricated buildings: prefabricated barn on Cranmoor Lodge Farm.

Perceptions of prefabricated buildings: Phoenix prefabs at Wake Green Road, Birmingham.

Perceptions of prefabricated buildings: Arcon Mk5 built 1946, Avoncroft Museum.

founded on personal valuations and empathies. For many, features and characteristics depicting poor robustness, sub-standard materials, shoddy construction techniques with poor quality of finishes signify some typical images and examples that remain lasting impressions of prefabrication. For others, prefabricated buildings rekindle immediate thoughts of a boring four-sided, single-storey, flat-roofed building, or box, that sits on the landscape like an incongruous lump. Prefabrication tends to conjure up, in the minds of some, a building devoid of a physical aesthetic worthy of merit and certainly lacking in any suggestion of architectural decorum. For others there is a dread of ever living in one. Anderson and Anderson

(2007, p. 8) refer similarly to preconceived notions surrounding prefabricated buildings: 'Stylistically, many people associate prefabrication with the simple forms, flat roofs, and minimalist detailing of modern buildings'. Architecture, however, surely is greater than this. Indeed, there has to be scope for far wider design thinking other than endorsing prefabrication as a quick-fix solution only and as responsible for a lack of design imagination and technical ingenuity.

The concept that surrounds prefabrication rests primarily in the potential for satisfying a need for a variety of accommodation types more quickly and in many instances with a measure of greater cost-efficiency. Churchill was alert to the need for an immediate response to the housing shortage and viewed prefabrication as an expedient answer to the situation that existed for industry and housing at that time (Vale, 1996). The situation is not too dissimilar today given that a huge demand for schools, factories, hospitals and the like continues. What is changing, however, albeit slowly and painfully, something akin to pulling teeth, is the recognition that prefabricated architecture, buildings and manufacturing all have a valid contribution to make, but there is a serious disconnect between all three. Government departments confirm they seek to deliver hundreds of thousands of new homes each year and boast about the vast sums of money they pledge to the same whilst manufacturers bemoan the lack of orders. Factory technology and manufacturing capacity already exist throughout the UK, with some factories having to concentrate on sourcing work rather than actively manufacturing. Architects are forever looking for work too but appear to fall shy of expanding their specialist design skills and expertise in prefabricated architecture but, at the same time, design and manufacturing expertise is always sought from companies outside the UK. The disconnect, therefore, can only be resolved by injecting the necessary glue to combine all of these disciplines as one entity as opposed to them operating in an interconnected vacuum.

Scale

Scale remains a fundamental feature in architecture. It has proved to be a feature of intense debate by architects, planners and theoreticians alike as they grapple with interpretation of architectural form, massing and scale, and with the relationship and interaction of the building specific parts to the whole and how the same might fit into the nature, extent and proportion of public open spaces forming the built environment. The common denominator for architectural appropriateness, however, often rests with 'human scale' and how the piece of architecture relates to its context.

Scale and Human Response to Scale

Within the mix and choices surrounding materials and how they might be arranged together, employing the myriad of technologies that are available to achieve the most appropriate design solution coupled with all the associated time- and cost-efficiencies, the human factor must also be considered. The human brain will translate its own interpretation and, depending upon its owner's own terms of reference, will decide whether the building is appropriate for its given culture and environmental context. The one common denominator that exists for all creeds and cultures is scale and the relevance of human scale will remain the deciding factor.

Section of prefabricated university building combining architectural and fabrication design in parallel.

Human Scale Reference

The value buildings have for the environment is measured by the manner in which humans react and interact within the environment those buildings create. There are always signs and signals that buildings provide in order that one may assess how and where they 'fit in'. The initial response to understanding buildings is steered by how they are acknowledged and read within their given context and is dictated by the ability of the human mind relating to its terms of reference: each will be different in some respect. Scale plays a significant role in allowing human perception to put together an appreciation of what buildings represent, but whether this has been successfully achieved by the architect is a different matter, irrespective of the abundance or constraints of financial budgets. What does matter, however, is the manner in which the place and buildings work for human interaction, personal benefit and well-being. Buildings can present an uplifting, overpowering, even a depressing experience but at all times the scale of the building and its surrounding environment will generate a human response which is dictated by the manner in which the building's elements are presented, both as a series of sub-elements and as a whole.

Human Perception

Reference was made in Chapter 1 to the classical order and the manner in which modularity, geometric order and scale when combined together offer up 'the whole'; that is, the total composition or the total entity. Whilst human consciousness generally allows 'human-scaled' aspects of the building to be coped with, it correlates with the physical make-up of its adjoining environment. However the building may be perceived, there can be difficulty in grasping the building's total entity as an overall composition and making sense of it. This can be due to the scale of a new physical entity being introduced. It usually refers to a dominant building appearing on the landscape or within a streetscape which can change personal terms of reference in relation to scale when reviewed against the height of familiar trees or adjoining buildings, or where a much-treasured view might hitherto have embraced a familiar sight-line or the ridge height of a mountain range that is now reduced or lost.

The perception of scale, therefore, and its relationship to buildings and the built environment will differ for each individual person and culture. A traditional vernacular tends to possess more human scale as the sizes of buildings being referred to are generally expected to be smaller in scale when compared to commercial structures of industrialized Western cultures.

The assembly and the size of the various elements, whether they form parts of a building or an assembly of buildings within a built environment, result in a total architectural composition. The juxtaposition of the parts to the whole represents the key for human interaction, as the proportions and size of the elements in relation to human scale will dictate the success or failure of the human experience. Interpreting the make-up of the buildings and the built environment within which they are placed will decide how successfully human capacity can organize, within the human consciousness, a rationale for acceptance or rejection. Decisions of this nature tend to refer back to the different cultures and terms of reference for each individual, consequently pure vernacular architecture of one culture will naturally be considered differently from one from a different society.

Architecture and Procurement Priorities

There has always been a debate between the construction and architectural fraternities surrounding the justification for art in architectural design. The architectural lobby in the main will maintain that the creation of a building without architectural design expertise or intellect will result in a building devoid of any real merit, meaning or value to mankind or community, or to the built environment within which it occupies a space and by default proclaims itself as a physical presence.

The construction delegation and manufacturing industrialists on the other hand will advocate the necessity for constructing and manufacturing efficiently and cost-effectively in order to achieve the objective. The emphasis here is usually on cost alone, where competition reigns among the construction and manufacturing fraternities. The art of architecture is often perceived as an 'add-on' and not affordable in the main. Applying a Philistine approach will provide little if any intelligent consideration as to how the building is intended to 'fit in' to its surrounding built environment or how its intended function will be satisfied, if the thrust of the exercise in the final analysis is merely to provide a building at minimum cost with minimum functionality. Clearly there are circumstances where the informed client will accept nothing other than a well-designed and considered building fit for the purpose for which it is intended. Similarly, the converse has a place from time to time too where the building requirement is for a covered space as quickly and at minimum cost but this too would enjoy the benefit of intelligent thinking surrounding design for which the architect is well qualified. Vale (1995, p. 37) acknowledges the validity of architectural influence by maintaining 'The appearance of a building does not depend primarily upon expense. Good planning, pleasant proportions and a careful choice of site and materials are far more important than cost. A capable architect can use even the cheapest materials with fine effect.'

The art of architecture is a design process embracing numerous facets, including how the building is to integrate with the natural and the built environments. These facets include site context, planning, building massing and scale, formation of spaces and spaces within a space, functionality, assembly options, methodologies and processes, current technology, materials, economics, people and communities, to name but a few. The architect's concept design process obliges him/her to undertake this responsibility seriously and to understand issues surrounding the design and delivery process for the same, within which PAMA has a valid claim.

Current Thinking on Prefabricated Architecture

Promoting PAMA to deliver a functional building as an architectural design solution might be perceived by some client funders and procurement officials as a risky enterprise on two fronts. In the first instance, the architect, whilst somewhat familiar with prefabrication and off-site processes generally, might not wish to risk the project with a delivery process where their specific knowledge and experience is founded more on the conventional construction methods and practices. Equally, some client funders and procurement officials, whilst familiar with the current hot conversations surrounding the off-site processes and prefabrication generally, are perhaps somewhat reluctant to instigate a move away from their more familiar choice of construction. Whilst they rightly suspect too that significant savings and efficiencies are to be achieved by employing prefabricated options and that it could be their perfect solution on many levels, a leap into the unknown for many is a leap too far. Notwithstanding the high level of debate and numerous facts, figures and surveys which demonstrate the benefits and attributes associated with prefabricated and modular buildings compared with conventional construction, there remains a reluctance to make that transition from conventional on-site build to off-site manufacturing (OSM) and assembly processes, especially at the project's concept design stage. It is, however, action at the concept design stage which is clearly preferable as this is where most time and cost benefit can be realized, up front. Whilst this appears to be a particular dilemma for public building procurement, indications suggest it is less so for privately funded projects and especially within the residential sector.

Adjusting to Change

The construction industry is not a discipline where change is sweeping and instant. Very often employing alternative modes of construction or adopting new technological applications and techniques is slow. This can be due to a preference to maintain the status quo for conventional build practices as opposed to adopting new methodologies and processes that have not been tried and tested enough for some clients, practitioners and professional contractors. This is difficult to justify, however, given the advances that have been made over the past ten years in particular. Equally, the reluctance among construction professionals and developers to adopt PAMA represents a project delivery process which is much too rapid, especially for the housing sector. It would mean current land banks held by the large national developers would become exhausted too soon and, more importantly, a pressing demand for housing would be eradicated sooner, which in turn would mean their land and house values would not grow with inflation over the longer time period, as appears to be the current strategy. This in itself does little to facilitate the housing shortage which currently prevails in the UK.

Manufacturers, on the other hand, tend to have a focus on delivering completed prefabricated buildings in the most expedient manner, employing the most advantageous technology with the honourable objective of making profit. Some off-site manufacturers seek to imply they possess the necessary in-house design skills for projects, irrespective of size and complexity as part of the package. This may be the situation in relation to the manufacturer's own particular system only but very few possess the necessary architectural design expertise in-house to dissect a client's brief and conceive a design solution suitable for progression through the RIBA work stages within a full design and build contract arrangement. That is not a manufacturer's specialism as matters tend to exist today and there is potential for a situation to arise that is not in the client's best interest, possibly with devastating consequences.

The ideal situation is for the trained architect to grasp and understand the essence of prefabricated manufacturing and assembly processes and practices as another design specialism. Prefabricated architecture necessitates architectural design philosophies to be applied which incorporate prefabricated technology and automation to understanding production lines and efficiencies. It will result in more enlightened design solutions where design innovation is automatic and with the prefabrication ethos lying at its core. Innovation and progressive thinking surrounding prefabricated architecture should remain current in the minds of those engaged in delivering buildings. It will take a brave building funder, decision-maker or a persuasive architect with PAMA design expertise, however, to instigate change in attitudes, to bend and unleash a new momentum.

Prefabricated architecture is not complicated. It revolves around a small number of simple concepts surrounding manufacturing assembly processes that already exist. Unfortunately, these options tend to operate in isolation and very often independently of one another; a prefabricated system might be selected for a project based on cost alone but without correct analysis or feasibility study to identify why a particular prefabricated system is appropriate (or not) for a given project. More in-depth consideration is given later (see Chapter 4), but for now it is worth identifying the underlying features within which prefabricated architecture is founded:

- panelized systems
- modularized systems (3D volumetric)
- hybrid construction – conventional construction plus panelization
- parts, components, sub-assemblies, complete assemblies, modularization.

Within all of these examples, prefabrication establishes itself as the common denominator. These examples originate from manufacturing processes which begin well in advance of them being required at the site, whether for a panelized installation or a modularized assembly. But, even prior to the manufacturing and assembly of the various prefabricated components, sub-assemblies and complete modular unit assemblies, an earlier process takes place. In order for every aspect of the completed building to

Automated panel assembly on a purpose-designed production line. (Courtesy of Frame Homes (SW) Ltd)

Modular building production on assembly line. (Courtesy of CIMC MBS Ltd)

be well thought out, an initial design process by way of a concept study with design options is carried out. The design process tests how best the functionality of the new building might be achieved for the various prefabricated systems being evaluated. Within the remit of a trained architect too, the environmental context will be examined in conjunction with other influencing factors. Given the nature of some buildings required and the awareness of the client for a ready-made solution, an architect may not be engaged for the project as the space requirements and arrangement, together with their respective interactions, do not generate any particular issue. In such a case, a simple order to a manufacturing company providing ready-made building solutions might suffice but this

would need to be done in the knowledge that the spaces provided are governed by the limitations of the selected manufacturer's particular system and not by the bespoke space requirements more fitting for the intended function perhaps. The tendency for clients with limited budgets to proceed with an order from a manufacturer direct is tempting but it often results in being a false economy.

Creating Time- and Cost-Efficiencies

Building projects of all types and sizes with varying levels of complexities have continued for many centuries and within the scope of building, associated risks will continue to evolve in parallel. It would be naive to suggest that construction projects can be designed and built without risk, and cost risk in particular. There is no scientific formula which accounts for every eventuality whereby all risk is identified and designed out from the project at the beginning. For instance, all sites are different with different features below ground and whilst the usual surveys will uncover most of what might be anticipated, there always remains a threat of an unknown presenting itself. Losing many cubic metres of concrete in a foundation pour might indicate shifting sand or an underground river not featured on any desktop study information. Underground cables or old mine

World's tallest modular apartment building, Croydon, UK. (Photo by author)

shafts, too, might be uncovered during excavations which will incur additional costs to circumvent the problem. The mission for every project, therefore, is to 'get out of the ground' as soon as possible, hopefully unscathed by significant events because once the substructure is complete the level of risk is reduced accordingly. This is a recognized fact proved many times over and, depending on the nature of the site, the provision of a sensible contingency sum in building contracts is a wise and prudent decision. The preference would be not to have to enter into the ground, but this is usually required for conventional construction. Designing out piling and deep trench foundations or minimizing excavations would prove to be a better option and for small- to medium-rise buildings prefabricated building solutions can facilitate this objective very effectively. Prefabricated high-rise buildings, however, are clearly different, necessitating different foundation solutions of a more robust nature, as in the case at 101 George Street, Croydon in the UK where the world's tallest modular apartment building is currently nearing completion.

Financial risk alone is not the dominant feature of any building project. A new building project has a myriad of features, characteristics and events which are not necessarily dictated by the size of the project alone. Indeed, all risk factors associated with building projects are inherent, but the skill is being able to identify potential risks and then knowing how to manage those risks. For an unseasoned client this can be a daunting undertaking. Managing risk includes assessing and evaluating an appropriate procurement route and in today's context there are two main contenders: the conventional route or the prefabricated route. Within the options available through prefabrication the ability to select a ready-made system build might appear attractive in terms of adhering to available budgets and of urgency in relation to preferred delivery dates. Where ready-made prefabricated building systems might be on the agenda for some, they generally tend to bypass the knowledge and expertise available from the architect or other professional consultants. Novice clients seem to have a propensity to make selections based on cost alone without fully appreciating what is and what is not included in the package and where the contractual pitfalls might lurk. Whatever procurement route is adopted the risk factor remains omnipresent which ultimately revolves around money.

The prospect for achieving cost-efficiencies in project delivery is forever gathering momentum. The quest for that magical solution, that undiscovered twist or angle to generate savings, whilst often imaginary, places new challenges on the design and construction personnel. Costs, however, are identified as two different entities and within the sphere of prefabrication especially are more achievable where professional expertise is involved in the project. They consist of 'time' cost, which is an entity in its own right, and then cost attributed to the actual building process. Both of these aspects overlap and impact on one another in many respects, the total of which can be identified as the 'project' cost. The diagram here sets out a simple overview for a usual situation for a typical project.

Time Cost

The issue of time is influenced by the speed at which the superstructure can be erected or, in the case of panelization, installed as part of a conventional construction process. Modular buildings, being a predominantly factory-based manufacturing process, require much less time on-site for the final assembly process at the site location. Time is calculated as an additional cost or saving to the project in a real and meaningful way. A sample project where time cost features as a saving would relate to a care home project, for instance, where a prefabricated design solution would seek to deliver the project perhaps some four to five months sooner than a conventional build project might be able to. This can be calculated from the outset, forming the strategy for the project. A typical care home project delivered in prefabricated architecture and accommodating up to sixty residents, each paying a fee of, say, around £800 per week, can thus realize savings close to £1m. Savings of this nature are relevant but, equally, where a delay in the project delivery occurs the financial situation is reversed. Moreover, with the ability to complete the project within a shorter time span further savings can be achieved from the main contractor's reduced preliminary costs. Preliminary costs are associated with the contractor managing the site and all the operations under his/her contract for the time he/she is on site.

Prefabricated architecture came to the rescue of another client's project originally designed as a conventional build solution but which proved to be non-viable due to excessive costs. Planning conditions dictated the management of major below-ground

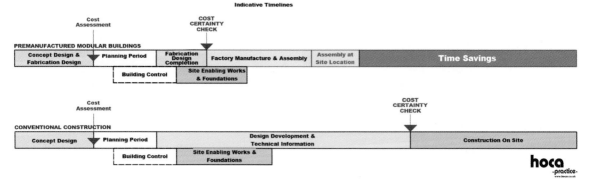

Timeline comparisons between modular buildings and conventional constructions. (Courtesy of HOCA Practice)

services; a culvert had to be installed to redirect an underground river; potential contamination existed given the history of the site and a significant piling element was insisted upon; all of which imposed significant costs and outstripped the financial capacity of the budget. By abandoning the conventional build approach and adopting a prefabricated design solution the below-ground enabling works were effectively designed out, substituting a simple concrete raft foundation. The concrete raft foundation provided a means of capping off the ground and leaving all below-ground issues undisturbed. Because the prefabricated superstructure was much lighter the depth of the concrete raft slab was kept to 150mm, with the perimeter depth at 600mm. This approach immediately designed out these significant planning conditions, thereby negating a massive expense to the project, and allowed the building process to commence unimpeded financially. Prefabricated architecture applied to this project provided a building which is able to accommodate a greater number of students within a slightly smaller building footprint and a significant reduction in project cost. More especially, an earlier delivery date allowed this client also to take advantage of an earlier intake of students and the accompanying fees.

Architectural Design Versus Manufacturing Expediency

Significant advances made in OSM technology and processes continue to open up new opportunities. Advances in prefabrication methods and techniques within the factory environment are at last allowing architects and designers to function with a greater level of design flexibility. This is in sharp contrast to previous perceptions held where prefabricated building in the UK was depicted as second-rate accommodation, originally intended to be temporary but functioning as a more permanent solution, even in its dilapidated state. There are many examples of early and mid-twentieth-century buildings that

remain within many parts of Europe where prefabricated components formed the mainstay of the design concept. For the UK government, the period after World War Two saw prefabrication as the big solution for solving the housing shortages. There is always a tendency for many of these temporary buildings to be retained well beyond their design life (Melbourne School of Design, 2011) due primarily to restricted budgets. Whilst the negative impact these early prefabricated structures made on the built environment is less than favourable, they nonetheless continue to carry a stigma that has discouraged many architects in the UK from embracing the formidable attributes prefabrication has to offer.

The early twentieth century saw a blind reluctance among UK architects to embrace standardized prefabrication and its associated disciplined rules of modularity. They appear to have been dissuaded from engaging in creating a new architecture for this medium with any measure of passion and determination, or perhaps it was the existence of certain restrictions and rigidity preventing design freedom surrounding space arrangement that caused architects to dismiss designing within the prefabrication ethos, predetermined by an inherent structural grid. Roth (1983) refers to the free plan being replaced by the modular plan and highlights the two notions as being totally opposite. He points out the rigid discipline associated with a modular plan being in opposition to the design of a free plan. Architects in practice today, however, and especially those more reliant on public sector commissions cannot afford to have the same lofty free plan ideals as those of previous generations. Equally however, prefabricated architecture design today is not restricted to the extent alluded to by Roth (1983). That said, architectural design can benefit where the economies of prefabricated manufacturing transition from the concept design process.

Taking Ownership

Prefabrication and its rapidly advancing technology have arrived at a stage where the opportunities for new markets are expanding fast. Housing alone is not the only urgency. The demand for intelligent hard-working prefabricated buildings is growing as design, manufacture and assembly become more dependent upon one another. It is incumbent upon architects to ensure that where buildings have a reliance on prefabrication they can only be as good as the demands placed on them (R.E. Smith, 2010). Smith goes on to highlight that where a reliance on fabrication is ignored, and especially by architects, a tendency for endeavours produced by off-site fabrication has less relevance within the architectural fraternity. This is to suggest that, without architectural design input, prefabrication can only be referred to as a building exercise devoid of design and

Altar rail mouse synonymous with Robert (Mouseman) Thompson (1876—1955) who was part of the 1920s revival in craftsmanship inspired by the Arts and Crafts movement.

architectural principles. Smith also advocates (2010, p. 335): 'For prefabrication to thrive as a building production, an understanding and implementation by architects and construction professionals into the processes is necessary.' What is more necessary is for architects to engage not only with concept design, as is the usual situation, but for the follow-through detail design process to include fabrication design in parallel, whether it consists of a panelized kit of parts or a complete three-dimensional volumetric modular entity.

The essence of prefabricated architecture is represented by its architecture, its fabrication processes and its aesthetic value for its given site context. It represents a significant shift away from adopting or employing the ubiquitous systems in isolation, merely as a quick-fix ready-made solution where space formation and arrangement is not dictated by architectural design but more by manufacturing protocols or personal preferences. In the current prefabrication renaissance, the level of interest and participation in prefabrication manufacturing technology is measurable but in small quantities only. For architects to succeed in this new quest, previously held perceptions of design limitations and restrictions must be abandoned as the potential for prefabricated architecture to be formalized as a design discipline is the aspiration to be realized. The architect's design and manufacturing skills therefore have to be joined up as a design specialism if a new arts and crafts movement in prefabricated and modular architecture is to be mobilized.

Design Flexibility

Prefabricated and modular technology has progressed significantly to allow architectural design expertise to introduce a new articulation into an architecture where current manufacturing processes are complementary. The capacity of a trained architect is capable of that. It has to be incumbent upon architects themselves, therefore, to assume the lead role in developing new concepts where prefabricated architecture results from the factory processes. Architects are expected to be architecturally literate and equipped to function effectively, with the ability to understand and appreciate the value of the built environment, its aesthetics and what is deemed to be a 'good fit' without surrendering to the off-the-shelf, helicopter drop-in approach.

Current Trends

Much of the answer lies in the fact that prefabricated buildings have for many years been devoid of any significant architectural design content in relation to enhancing the aesthetic of the built environment, their function in relation to human activity and integration, or indeed their suitability and value in relation to contributing to green sustainable buildings. Current trends in demand and the significant advances in prefabricated manufacturing technology of late act as the main catalysts for meeting design aspirations. New building demands have always had a focus on housing, and issues surrounding robustness and mortgageability remain uppermost in the minds of many, from the prospective mortgagee to the mortgagor. At the same time concepts of permanent building solutions, waste reduction, superior quality and reduced time with on-site activities remain. For prefabricated architecture to reinforce its status among the design fraternity in the first instance, and among clients ultimately, design needs to be all-embracing. It must accommodate the buildings' architecture, fabrication and manufacturing processes, transportation and site installation or assembly as an integral element of the final design solution and not as an external sub-element as is current today. Design must also demonstrate its ability to take its place in the built and natural environments where its aesthetics must not only be equal but preferably a marked enhancement to that which it replaces. The scope for architects to take greater ownership of total design surrounding prefabricated architecture is omnipresent and immense. It represents a larger remit for architects which is naturally reflected in business opportunities recognized by only very few architects and then mostly not within the UK. The industrialist

and manufacturer, however, in many ways continue to be more alert to the evolving market, the constant budget constraints and the urgency of time placed on building projects by clients and less so by architects, regretfully, who could be seen as playing catch-up.

Current focus is now on the progress made by the industrialist off-site manufacturers and large construction companies who have recognized a potential for significant business opportunities. As a result, they have set up their own OSM facilities, all answering the urgent demands of the last two decades. Due to the huge financial constraints placed on government and local government budgets, sectors beyond the housing urgency are also under serious consideration for employing prefabricated and modular solutions. The focus of clients and manufacturers has always been on time- and cost-efficiencies and as current trends unfold one can only suggest the architects' focus must become sharper. If architects are to remain germane, they need to include prefabricated designed solutions as one of the first considerations within their concept design stage analysis. Their engagement with the prefabricated design process from the very beginning will maintain the architectural influence over prefabricated architecture design, as opposed to slavishly adopting the outcomes from options where mechanization alone is the arbiter.

Manufacturers' Design Approaches

The main thrust lying behind the ability to manufacture total wall, floor and roof panels in a prefabricated process rests with the advances in machine technology. Some might argue that factory processes are led by the requirements of architectural design where the design process instigates new technology. Others, however, support the theory that it is existing factory conventions and processes which act as the catalyst for the design concept where the resulting design solution naturally embraces current factory capabilities as the default position, dictating ultimately what is and what is not possible. Irrespective of which contributory element is placed at the forefront, the ability to achieve particular design solutions by means of factory technological options available remains the primary consideration. 'All such trends ultimately make economic sense if they improve performance: that is if they result in cheaper buildings of better quality with greater durability' (Sebestyén, 1998, p. 151). Within the scope of prefabrication there is an urgency which occupies specialist fabrication designers, constructors and off-site manufacturers alike and that is to satisfy functional requirements in the most expedient and economical manner as a prerequisite, thereby making the building affordable. This is where many prefabricated building projects differentiate between an architectural design solution and merely a building exercise.

The core element surrounding prefabrication and modular design for the future is the architect's ability to engage in architectural design for a factory culture. As a first step, architects themselves must identify architectural solutions through prefabricated systems that already exist and seek to innovate further in conjunction with appreciating the manufacturing processes involved. They need to be appropriately skilled in fabrication design, sufficiently acquainted with manufacturing and assembly processes at the factory, together with recognizing site installation and assembly methodologies in order to present prefabricated architecture as a totally holistic solution to meet current demands. Succeeding with this goal is fundamental for achieving bespoke design solutions and for prefabricated architecture to become a meaningful design solution for clients. Collaborative design and manufacturing strategies between architects and manufacturers therefore is the next step to demonstrate to clients and government procurement officials alike how full advantage of the cost benefits and time savings are to be realized.

Sustainability

Since time began planet Earth has provided for almost all of humankind's needs and wants but there are now more and more indicators to suggest the increase of the human population and activity coincides with the depletion of our natural resources. Human activities on Earth are represented through an array of different cultures and societies, some of which draw a larger share of Earth's resources or discharge gases and pollutants which are totally out of scale with neighbouring human activity. To endure, humankind needs to make some changes. The catalyst surrounding this level of contamination is always business and commercial enterprise and whilst the activities and practices of the Industrial Revolution launched the Western world into economic prosperity the environmental cost cannot be sustained at the same rate. As a global society the need to transform our markets has to be identified. Within the UK we continue to focus on how to produce and consume in a more sustainable manner. Equally, the very ways in which we define and measure value and progress have to be reassessed in the current global context. This is a huge quest, and one that does not just revolve around business and economics. It necessitates an enormous social, political, technological, cultural and behavioural transformation for governments too; their need to motivate by inducement and to set targets and rules for a level playing field would be a reasonable objective.

Designing sustainable buildings, sometimes referred to as 'green buildings', does not revolve around just any one aspect or process. Due to the complexities and multitude of processes and considerations involved in a building project, from the initial design concept stage to completion on-site, it is difficult for any one individual to have complete possession of all these ingredients and be equipped to provide a magic bullet solution. Clearly, no such solution exists. What does exist, however, is a growing level of research and practical knowledge which identifies and highlights many of the aspects and ingredients which are involved in construction processes and which of these tend to offer a better choice in terms of designing and building, or designing and manufacturing, greener and more sustainable buildings.

Current research indicates that the benefits of greener buildings are clear and relate more to buildings where human activity occurs, such as schools, hospitals, residential housing and other community buildings. Many of the features discussed by Ford (2007) highlight the importance of design features such as the building's orientation to the sun, fountains providing evaporation and cooling, cisterns that recycle water and the siting of the building to reduce wind resistance, to name but a few. Within this mix is the inclusion of materials, which Ford cites for one of the schools discussed as being sourced locally 'to minimize cost and environmental impact'. It is unlikely that prefabrication will be able to contribute to sustainability to this degree as most of the materials employed in prefabricated building are sourced away from the site location as the fabrication occurs within a factory environment located in one place. From the one factory location, however, the scope for producing completed modular buildings and modular units provides a superior contribution to 'green buildings' when compared to the overall activities of a conventional construction process on-site.

It is recognized that prefabrication does not have a direct connection with the design features referred to by Ford as these relate to the core design decisions by the architect during the design concept stage. Within the context of prefabricated building, however, the selection of materials and fabrication methodologies at the concept design stage are significant; such choices dictate the level of sustainability that is considered and designed into the building from the beginning. Valuable credits for Building Research Establishment Environmental Assessment Method (BREEAM) ratings can also be achieved at this initial stage of the project. Prefabrication has the capacity to demonstrate to the BREEAM assessor how factory-produced buildings can generate less water usage, less pollution, less wastage of materials, less energy, less disturbance to the ecology and improved health, safety and well-being when compared to the multitude of site activities and traffic movements normally associated with a conventional build project.

Aesthetics

Aesthetics by Design

Architectural design and aesthetics are emotive topics. They can inaugurate a feud in an architect's mind when assessing design priorities in the context of client objectives, goals and aspirations. The battle

Aesthetic beauty of the Viceroy butterfly.

for the aesthetic is very often competing against an ambitious brief with a restricted budget. Some project participants who are less preoccupied with design, perhaps, might suggest that aesthetics relate to ideas of what is visually appealing based on personal terms of reference, emotions and beliefs and that anything outside of this notion has no validity. The pragmatists within the project team, however, might be equally convinced in their beliefs. They may be adamant that for a building to justify its existence, the first prerequisite must be affordability, lest the building might never materialize, and so a focus on functionality alone is sufficient rather than no building at all. Clearly the character and personality of a building is shaped by many unique influences and deeply held views by some, each of which will have a unique impact on the building's life and soul.

When the analysis and soul-searching is complete the very essence of the building's DNA is distilled into two principal features. First, the building has a beginning which usually commences with a concept surrounding what the building might look like, in which case the concept is engaging at an aesthetic level. In the second instance, the initial concept is born out of a need for a building to perform a specific function only, in which case the manner in which the building is constructed has greater significance and will usually be dictated by the method of procurement, with or without formal design consideration.

Accordingly, for some the aesthetic is referenced by their culture as it represents aspects of visual connection, features and detail that are familiar and comfortable for them, and has a natural appeal to their senses. It could be a sense of emotional connection and belief founded upon terms of reference that are familiar and innate. For others the ingredients for good taste might well be an understanding and appreciation of form and massing, colour and texture, proportion, symmetry and the like. In all of these representations and many others besides, the idea of beauty (or ugliness) is conveyed in the language used to describe sentiments surrounding the aesthetic, characterizing perception in relation to the human

form, art, music or architecture, for instance. In all matters associated with the aesthetic there are rules, although these may have a measure of unpredictability or a capacity to excite anticipation and even expectation. They define an order and discipline that are recognizable, around which a connection and relationship are maintained.

In order to explain this a bit further, reference to the structural order of music is appropriate. Within the confines that surround tonality, say, a piece of music could be deemed to represent an exclusive pattern embracing melody and chords. Hearing such music at first can register unpredictability while at the same time it maintains the hierarchy of form and tonality. Mozart's genius, it is said, lay in the manner in which he divorced himself from the rules that prevailed at the time. Instead he redefined tonality by presenting it against a measure of discord as in the 'Dissonance' Quartet (P.F. Smith, 2003). By doing so Mozart introduces a new order by displaying a creative collision between order and complexity, thereby expanding the frontier of aesthetic potential in a musical context.

As in music, when architecture detaches itself from the normal rules, a measure of randomness ensues and consequently the opportunity for perceiving a level of organization and patterned order is almost non-existent. For example, when the predictable repetitiveness of standardized modularity is interrupted by a random element a measure of welcome relief is inevitable by such unpredictability. In the context of music and architecture, then, when a piece of art fails to grasp any comprehension of organization and order the usual effect is measured in ugliness and dismissal. In contrast, strict symmetrical and balanced order in pattern, devoid of visual excitement and stimulation, fails to extract a worthwhile aesthetic response. This is due primarily to the absence of any essential bare minimum of unpredictability or complexity to be resolved through a design process. In other words, and in an architectural context, the mystery of anticipation and excitement are vital ingredients to initially stimulate and ultimately generate a basic appreciation of aesthetic. If this randomness ingredient is absent from an ordered composition the result can be mundane, ordinary perhaps, and even dull or uninteresting.

Aesthetics Through Manufacture

Understanding aesthetics in relation to rules of organization was not a design philosophy applied by industrialists to prefabrication in the early twentieth century when playing a role in solving the housing shortages. Their priorities were different. In essence, design for the industrialist tended to have a focus on efficient manufacture with a clear emphasis on mass-produced standardized products. This primary objective naturally followed through in employing the same products to create mass-produced standardized buildings under the same efficiency ethos. Standardization as a vehicle for unitized housing, especially, was a byword for seeking to address the housing shortages throughout the twentieth century but with little if any reference to aesthetics in an architectural context.

Whilst housing shortages continue into the twenty-first century similar approaches to manufacturing unitized housing remain but under a new terminology identified as modular building. There appears to be a mild acceptance in present-day examples of prefabricated modular housing, perhaps due more to the increasing urgency, but whether this is based on an appreciation for the aesthetic or a preference for affordable housing has not been fully tested. Irrespective of any sentiments towards design style or aesthetics, there is, however, much less willingness by major house builders and housing associations to engage in a meaningful way with prefabricated and modular architecture. Feeble attempts are made with small housing projects, if only to indicate some interest in and compliance with government directives towards OSM but aspects surrounding aesthetics appear not to be part of the mix. Irrespective of the benefits prefabricated and modular architecture have to offer the uptake is limited primarily by historic

perceptions associated with prefabrication. The standard response to OSM and prefabricated architecture is that aesthetics will be stifled as a result; this is untrue and whilst there will always be an appetite for iconic buildings it should not be taken to mean a high-quality aesthetic does not prevail for housing, schools and infrastructure (House of Lords Report, 2017–19).

House builders are particularly singled out for special mention in the House of Lords Report, (2017–19, p. 25), where the 'current culture and structure of the construction sector is not conducive to extensive use of off-site manufacture, placing barriers in the way of wider uptake'. The major house builders, on the other hand, will cite reasons of lack of volume and project commitment by government and social landlords in OSM to make it financially viable and, indeed, there is a measure of validity in that too. Until some level of equilibrium is established between those purporting to be responsible for housing provision the notion of aesthetic in prefabricated architecture might have to take a back seat for a little time longer within the existing regime.

Design: The Science and Technology Aesthetic

For many centuries the building and construction industries have always been a haven for the craftsperson connected with all facets of the construction process. Architects, too, have always had a good understanding of what is achievable to produce the best solution in the design output. Understanding detail design of the building and what is possible from craftspeople today has greater relevance, given the stress placed on skilled tradespersons and their training. Where building becomes a product from the factory, architects must also demonstrate a level of competency in the new science of building through prefabricated and modular architecture and the manufacturing processes associated with the same. 'The first organization of architects stated that their purpose was to promote "architectural science"' (R.E. Smith, 2010, p. 24). Whilst a certain amount

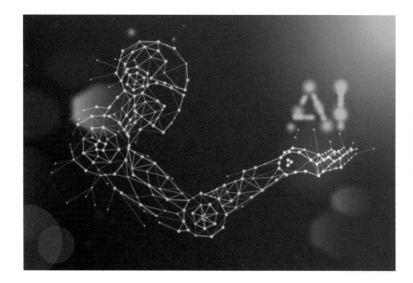

Computer vision is much faster than that of humans in some well-defined recognition tasks.

of reskilling is required for the new manufacturing processes, architects also need to demonstrate an equal appreciation of evolving new skills relating to current manufacturing and assembly processes and how the same can result in the most advantageous solution for their designs.

Innovative and imaginative building projects are created by matching these same qualities in design strategies. Therefore, the architect must seek to produce a bespoke design whilst adopting standardization by design; that is, designing for manufacture and assembly (DfMA) within the emerging automation and artificial intelligence (AI) applications. It naturally follows that with the advent of science and new manufacturing technologies a host of new factory skills currently being applied to manufacturing are also on the increase. Architects, whilst part of an established profession, must keep abreast with what is under constant review within the factory environment. Fostering proficiency in design skills in every aspect of PAMA is now crucial for this design specialism to be one which the architect must own, lest architectural design in prefabrication become totally obsolete. For architects to remain with some 'skin in the game' it is for the architectural profession to embrace the emerging technologies of automation and artificial intelligence (AI) associated with factory manufacturing and assembly processes as a integral

part of their concept design process and delivering prefabricated buildings. One could look at how the fashion industry, with its own well-established fraternity of designers and manufacturers, recognizes that AI is already emerging in transforming fashion design and manufacture and the way in which fashion is now marketed and sold.

Industrial Design Prevails

Introduction

Creating a building on a parcel of land usually referred to as 'the site' embraces many tried and tested techniques that have evolved over many centuries in conjunction with employing a myriad of locally available materials. From humankind's earliest placing of one stone on top of another in order to create an enclosure, to current-day standards and expectations employing highly sophisticated assemblies of man-made materials, we can see humankind's resolve, innovativeness and invention. Creating similar human enclosures today, albeit of a very different nature and scale perhaps, and for a more wide-ranging set of reasons relating to human activity, involves a constant and ever-evolving process that continues to this day. The concept surrounding 'building construction' in today's global environment represents many centuries of enterprise, experience, know-how and especially innovativeness. Industrial invention is gripped by innovative design and with it a design philosophy as it reflects the times to which it relates. These represent just a few of the vital ingredients generally considered to be the principal features that surround an ever-evolving building industry and, depending on one's point of view, its impact and influence on the built environment.

In recent years prefabrication has enjoyed a resurgence in status and recognition, primarily due to the advances in factory production methods, technology and techniques. Even more significant in these tough economic times is the urgency for buildings to be delivered in a greener and more time-efficient and cost-effective manner. Consequently, the refined prefabrication processes can now deliver prefabricated buildings as a total design and build solution (turnkey) as opposed to only employing prefabricated components and sub-assemblies as individual and separate entities normally associated with conventional construction. By inference, prefabricated building offers itself as a vehicle for fostering a higher-quality architecture as a result, especially where a more holistic approach to architectural design is employed by the trained architect as part of the total process. There is now a move away from the previously held view associated with the term 'prefab' which hitherto represented 'makeshift' temporary classrooms, bungalows, domestic garages or indifferent precast building blocks. As with 'standardization', the driving force lying behind new prefabrication technology and its resulting architecture in current times is shared between cost- and time-efficiencies as a first priority. However, R.E. Smith (2010) identifies the significance and necessity for architectural designers and thinkers to take responsibility for embracing standardization and prefabrication and apply the same in relation to three-dimensional forms that represent our culture and built environments: 'Architects need to develop an understanding of the history, theory and pragmatics of prefabrication so they may effectively develop and implement these methods into the production of architecture'.

Design Influence and the Manufacturing Process

Following World War One there was an urgency for promoting mass prefabrication solutions and techniques in the UK when sufficient housing could not be met by the more traditional building methods due primarily to the shortfall of the trades systems. Given the extent of the housing shortage following World War One and the ever-increasing housing

Post-war prefabs: nearly 200 of these single-storey prefabricated houses in asbestos, cement and timber were erected on the Downham Estate in Lewisham in 1948.

shortage accruing between the two wars, by 1945 the housing requirement became even more acute resulting from the bombing and the lower priority dedicated to housing during hostilities. At the end of the war, factories previously engaged in full production for the war effort now faced the prospect of reduced armaments production which necessitated a measure of creative thinking by replacing their armaments production with some other profitable enterprise. Their ability to undertake factory manufacturing process remained ever-present but their capacity to engage in production surrounding traditional house building practice and materials such as timber and brickwork posed a different challenge. As a result of their efficient wartime production capabilities, where manufacturing prowess already prevailed, their ability to undertake prefabricated housing was perceived to be well within their capability.

The Ministry of Works instigated standards for all approved prefabricated units, providing a minimum standard floor area and a maximum width to facilitate road transportation. The accommodation was termed as a 'service unit' by the Ministry of Works, where a back-to-back kitchen and bathroom arrangement was created within the factory environment: this sought to accommodate unsightly plumbing and electrical installations within the same zone. Under the Housing Act the Ministry of Works was responsible for realizing a total of 156,623 temporary prefabricated houses during the period 1945–51, all with magnolia walls and their joinery and doors painted a gloss green. Not all of the new occupants warmed to prefabricated homes as the perception, even then, was that they were considered to be inferior to the more traditional permanent built homes irrespective of any architectural design merit or attributes which may or may not have been in evidence.

The manufacturing industrialist, however, will tend to be less concerned about any aesthetic implications as these can be replaced by the beauty of engineering within the architectural context. The Crystal Palace was a prime example of precision engineering but equally, and almost by default, its exquisite

engineering produced a highly acclaimed piece of architecture. Salingaros and Tejada (2001) refer to how modular arrangements often define the aesthetics of a 'style'. The crux of the debate surrounding current trends for present-day prefabricated building is the extent to which future architectural design will embrace panelized and modularized prefabrication technology and techniques to encourage further architectural gems like the Crystal Palace to evolve. In pursuance of design aesthetics within the standardized prefabrication ethos, one needs to examine what should be the catalyst for standardized prefabrication in manufacturing and what should attract architects to design their 'free plan' ideas within this disciplined geometry. Will it mean adhering strictly to design principles instigated by modular geometry for manufacturing expediency, or holding fast to past generations of architectural design principles and thinking, or is there a soft pink line over which 'toe-dipping' in design can occur from time to time?

Central to prefabricated architecture succeeding in today's housing, education, health and commercial sectors is its ability to demonstrate an architecture by way of a design philosophy where the final design solution embraces the very core of architectural design principles in conjunction with factory assembly and manufacture processes, all as a joined-up exercise, beginning at the concept design stage of a project. Knapp (2013) refers to a history of false starts in furthering prefabrication as an architectural discipline and also suggests that ideals surrounding standardization and systemization were more readily embraced by other industries. More to the point, perhaps, is the suggestion that architects adopted a mindset of aloofness from the manufacturing process, thereby abandoning risk and responsibility to developers and builders where profit is a prerequisite for any sustainable business. An OSM industry already exists within the UK but it continues to seek greater government commitment to volume production in order to satisfy continuing demand for mass housing for the twenty-first century and to create and sustain viable business opportunities for a new science in prefabrication. For prefabricated architecture to become a recognized design discipline it requires the commitment of architects, especially, to engage in this design specialism where aligning architectural design with manufacturing and assembly processes is the accolade.

Modular Buildings and Architectural Design Influence

Prefabrication as an industrial technology only resulted from the new revolutionary techniques of the mid-1880s. It is only in the last twenty years, however, and within the UK especially, that premanufactured modular buildings have been identified by some architects and promoted by the modern-day industrialist as a viable alternative to conventional

Architectural geometry in modular buildings.

construction, citing quality and cost- and time-efficiencies as the principal motivators. In conjunction with these elements, modular premanufactured buildings are being examined more closely for their design status and architectural identity, thereby necessitating a new architectural language or style which, however, struggles to be identified in relation to prefabrication generally and modular buildings in particular, where the building's architectural geometry resides and is perhaps more obvious. Architectural geometry embraces the combination of applied geometry with architecture where the actual geometry functions as a nucleus around which the architectural design in modular manufacture and assembly processes is evaluated. The 'Gherkin' in London is an example of how architecture can refer to geometry but then imitate natural forms that are then standardized and reproduced as modularized façades and modular buildings.

The thrust behind all architectural compositions consists of a number of elements that define the structural grid in the first instance, and thereafter the sub-elements, that reside within the grid's geometry. The visual connection for the human brain rests with reading the scale of both the sub-elements and main elements of the building's architecture, the whole of which forms the total aesthetic. The architectural quality may be measured by the manner in which the

Architectural geometry in modular façades: The Gherkin, London.

human being identifies with the order, proportions and rhythm set out by the architect but unless this is self-explanatory and distinct it can only sensibly be considered in relation to one's own terms of reference, culture and knowledge.

In examining modular buildings and their architecture as two separate individual entities there is a tendency to perceive architecture in the context of an aesthetic and for a building as a feat of technological accomplishment; that is, as a building exercise. Indeed, there is validity in both as the technology, when expressed as part of the physical appearance of the building, almost becomes integral to the architecture. In many ways, too, the technological features of the building can easily form the essence of the architecture which when intentional is acceptable but, for some, is often less so in relation to the building's aesthetic. Consequently, there can be a dilemma in trying to decipher the aesthetic from the building's architecture and its technology. Debate will always be induced when seeking to rationalize which elements of the completed building represent the architecture expressing the aesthetic against what indicates the essence of the building's assembly process and the technology employed. In the final analysis, the object for any building is to present itself to its immediate and wider environmental context as a display of harmony within which beauty is the core. This clearly is achieved in many instances by a display of both of these features in total harmony. Beyond the building's architecture and aesthetic lie a number of other features which the design process must rationalize; these are very often in conflict with one another for priority status, such as the brief, planning requirements, budget and ground conditions, all of which come under the direction of the architect and his/her design principles and style preference. Harmony is an expression that is liberally employed in relationship to architecture even though its origins might derive from a music reference, perhaps. A clear understanding of what harmony represents in music might exist more readily than might prevail within an architectural context. (*See also* the earlier discussion in this chapter under the heading 'Aesthetics'.)

Responding to the Market

It is only in the last twenty years that the attributes associated with prefabricated buildings within the construction industry have presented themselves as viable alternatives to the more conventional construction practices. Spearheading the concept of prefabrication, manufacture assembly processes remain an omnipresent quest to economize on cost and time where time in itself has a related cost. Prefabrication, though, is not a new phenomenon, as the first principles surrounding factory-manufactured building components emerged as a result of the technological advances made during the Industrial Revolution.

Under the umbrella of prefabrication lie numerous adaptations and applications, each striving for prominence within the marketplace by offering its own unique attributes as valid reasons why a particular system is superior to others. So why has no one particular prefabricated system outshone any other and evolved into the absolute panacea to solve all design and project issues usually associated with the building process? The answer is simple. There is no single remedy, system or process associated with prefabrication that can present itself as the absolute answer as none exists either for conventional building. Modern prefabrication technology and progressive assembly processes when applied to the overall building process can satisfy the majority of demands called for within a building project, but no one magic system solution has yet been invented and nor will it ever do so in the evolutionary process that is architecture. Options surrounding stick-build, open panel, closed panel, and structural insulated panel with their associated building systems already exist, as do systems for modular buildings. It is down to the skill of the architect and the professional team to assess the site and determine the most appropriate solution for the given circumstances. Understanding the options available and their manufacturing and assembly processes, together with a total grasp of the design brief and end user requirements, is crucial for a successful PAMA design solution.

Past references and future trends for prefabricated buildings tend to revolve around the housing market. Research and driver indicators rely on this particular sector to evaluate the potential for future markets. It is this sector on which manufacturers based the viability of their businesses, but at the same time being ever ready to entertain opportunities from other sectors. In relation to the housing market the Roland Berger Report (2018) highlights a number of preferences and differences between traditional build and prefabricated build projects. For example, their report indicates walls within conventional built houses are considered to be more secure than prefabricated build, prefabricated housing solutions tend to offer a greater price certainty and whilst customized architectural design has improved, conventional build houses notwithstanding appear to offer less technical constraints.

Current UK government initiatives are seeking to attract new entrants into the UK housing market in an attempt to deliver around one million homes by 2025. In examining this objective against past performance of both the construction sector (whose members tend to prefer the traditional build approach) and the government's commitment to large volume housing projects there continues to be an unbridgeable disparity. There is, however, scope for delivering the one million houses where a shift of emphasis is taken from the established 'big player' house building fraternity and a greater investment provided to an already established manufacturing industry specializing in prefabricated building which is seeking to expand its business but which can only happen if its participants secure a part of the orders. The UK has already witnessed the impact associated with government placing total and absolute reliance on the 'big player' regime so there is real justification for a greater confidence being placed on the smaller enterprise companies and spreading risk. Other countries in Europe already have an established house manufacturing industry where clients and customers identify with the manufacturer builder as a natural first choice. For now, in the UK, the focus continues to be on the 'big players' setting up new multimillion pound facilities which, up till now, seem to be engaged in setting up the facility.

Chapter Three

Fabricating the Architecture

Introduction

Architectural design tends to remain isolated from the fabrication design process associated with prefabricated and modular architecture. Moreover, there appears to be a determined effort to maintain the status quo for retaining traditional practice where both the conventional construction activities and design thinking remain as two separate and distinct disciplines. In his oral evidence to the House of Lords Select Committee on Science and Technology, Bew (2018) refers specifically to the lack of the design expertise necessary for designing for manufacture and highlights that if you (as a client) 'go to a traditional architect or engineer, you are likely to get a traditional result'. The disconnect between architectural design and fabrication design has remained for decades whereby a continuous lacuna prevails between the two disciplines. The challenge for the architect, therefore, is first to recognize that design specialisms associated with prefabrication and its manufacture and then to engage where designing for manufacture and assembly is an integral part for the overall architecture design solution.

Prefabricated and Modular Architecture (PAMA)

Building Procurement Options

Prefabricated and modular architecture (PAMA) buildings essentially consist of two distinct assembly processes, both of which are commonly referred to as modular. Depending on the client's design brief for a specific building, the site characteristics, together with a plethora of other contributing features associated with the project and the architect's concept design process will inform which factory assembly and site installation processes for either three-dimensional (3D) volumetric or two-dimensional (2D) panelization will be the most appropriate.

Where the concept design delivers a design solution defining volumetric as most suitable for a given set of criteria, the project can benefit further

Premanufactured SIP roof cassette used as a modular component in prefabricated panelized construction. (Courtesy of Kingspan Timber Solutions Ltd)

by including within the total design and assembly process a completely fitted-out volumetric component, sometimes referred to as a modular unit or component. There are clear advantages in procuring a building through the volumetric route as much of the assembly for the building is completed within a factory environment, leaving only the final assembling of the modular units for the site location. Completed volumetric units might consist of a total floor level of a family house or half an apartment's floor area or a third of a classroom. They can include all internal and external walls, floor and ceiling structure and finishes, all electrical, plumbing and data installations, and complete bathroom and kitchen installations, leaving only the final connections to central duct locations to be completed as part of the on-site assembly process. Significant time savings result from this method as the main contractor on the site can undertake and complete the on-site foundations and below-ground services installation whilst at the same time the volumetric assembly process is under way within the factory.

Panelized assembly on the other hand is restricted to the manufacture of wall panels or floor and roof cassettes, referred to earlier as sub-assemblies and components. They are delivered from the factory to the site without finishes and merely form part of the on-site construction process, primarily as a set of prefabricated structural walls and floors. In essence, this is referred to as panelized construction mainly because most of the activities on the site continue to consist of construction activities similar to a conventional form of construction where the panelized walls, floors and roof form a specialist sub-contractor package. Whilst panelized construction (also referred to as prefabricated building) can generate some time savings for the project it cannot be compared in a meaningful way with the volumetric (modular) assembly and site assembly process. The different benefits and attributes that exist between volumetric/modular buildings and panelized construction are easily measured by the amount of off-site activities associated with each of the two options. A more efficient project development can be better realized through the volumetric modular process where all the advantages of quality assurance, time certainties and working environments are more readily available.

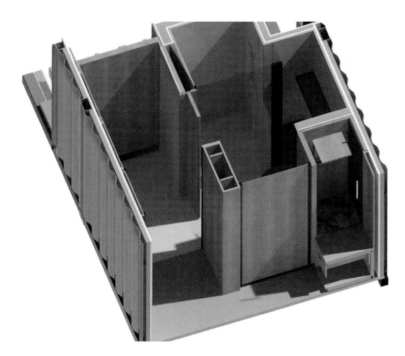

Modular bedroom unit with internal fit-out for hotel, Bristol, UK. (Courtesy of CIMB MBS Ltd)

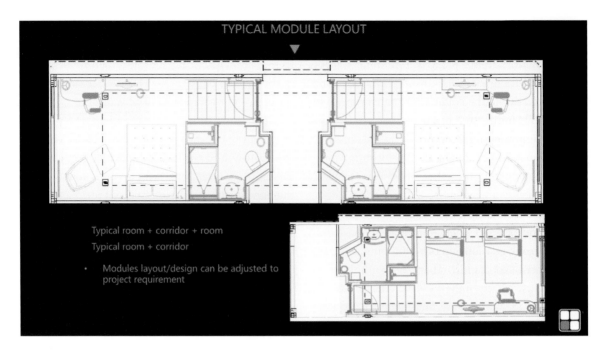

Plan of modular unit accommodating two bedroom suites and a central corridor. (Courtesy of CIMC MBS Ltd)

Cost Implications Versus Aesthetic Preferences

Continuous pressures placed on design and construction teams to generate greater time- and cost-efficiencies is not new. However, since the beginning of the economic downturn in the UK in 2008, client funders tasked with managing central and local government budgets have generated a new focus on building procurement where more building is expected for the same money, and sometimes even less. New demands are placed on professional teams to manage the design process with a keen efficiency where materials are used, and the construction methods employed demonstrate greater efficiency both in terms of time and cost. In following the more conventional procurement route, all too often projects are taken through the design process of developing the concept design, and sometimes even to a more detailed design status, only to discover the budget cannot cope with the project's costs. This naturally results in a huge rethink surrounding the viability of the project or, indeed, whether the project can be saved but at a reduced cost. Usually, within this reappraisal environment the project might be considered a candidate for an off-site manufacturing (OSM) solution but its architecture will become something of a hybrid through necessity and devoid of any design purity as a result. In other words, it is difficult to see how a completed building originally designed with a conventional architectural design solution in mind can retain its architecture and aesthetic preferences where elements of off-site manufacture are introduced later, primarily to satisfy a budget but without the full benefits of OSM being realized. A PAMA design solution, however, where a total end-to-end design philosophy is employed at concept design stage so as to maximize the full benefit in terms of cost- and time-efficiencies, will naturally facilitate a more precise architecture.

Prefabrication Science

Unlike in the UK and in Europe generally where the art of design remains the principal focus for architects, in America architects may have become the victim of a disservice by the cultivation of a very close association with the science of building. As a consequence, society and architectural practitioners have seen that architectural education and training can only sensibly be delivered through systematic methods, unlike in the UK. R.E. Smith (2010, p. 24) goes on to infer that at the time of the Enlightenment the architectural fraternity in America sought to align their activities with those of doctors and other practising scientists whose work was founded more on scientific practice. Leopold (2006) highlights the major void that exists between the arts and sciences and highlights, too, how the strong relationship between geometry and architecture becomes lost. There is good reason to believe, therefore, given the connection to science in the practice of the art of architecture, the advances America made in prefabricated building, technology and techniques seem to surpass those applied within the UK generally, where architects, for all their preoccupation in the art form alone, appear to have failed to grasp the capacity to apply the art of architectural design to the science of standardization and prefabrication for their architecture. (*See* Chapter 5 under the heading 'Precast Concrete Panels'.)

Managing PAMA Delivery

Over the past two decades especially, the rapid advances in prefabrication, technology and machine automation have been instrumental in identifying alternative procurement options for project funders with ever-restricted budgets. The core elements of this new design environment have resulted mainly from the development of materials, products and component assemblies coupled with new simplistic on-site construction and installation methods. The advantages associated with PAMA are becoming more familiar to the design and construction fraternities, albeit at a slower pace than many within the OSM industry would prefer. Much of this slow pace, however, can be attributed to the lack of total commitment for government-funded projects and

to the low level of volumes that would make it sensible and financially viable. Off-site manufacturers forever decry the lack of volume as clients and building funders tend to 'toe-dip' with their commitment to OSM. Clients and building funders may be forgiven for their reticence and restraint in committing in a meaningful way when design expertise and commitment to prefabricated architecture is not forthcoming from their architects and construction professionals.

Buildings procured through PAMA methodologies, science and technology will always continue to have a significant influence within the OSM environments. The most effective way of managing and delivering PAMA, therefore, should be for architects to be more engaged and understanding of the total end-to-end manufacturing process as a natural part of their concept and detail design strategy in the first instance. Indeed, there is scope for architects to create a capacity for developing their concept design founded on design for manufacture and assembly (DfMA) principles as opposed to accepting surrender due to budget necessities or merely accepting a pre-defined solution on offer from the off-site manufacturer as a fait accompli. When engaged at the front end of prefabrication design, architects as research practitioners in PAMA would secure a superior knowledge and expertise which would be considered a prerequisite to becoming well-rounded in panelization and modularization design specialism. In the present environment of value-for-money design solutions, architectural training needs to include some provision for prefabrication within their training programmes (as is the situation within fashion design, for instance). Students of architecture need to be introduced to the core principles of prefabricated and modular architecture design as a natural element for well-considered prefabricated design solutions. Formal architectural training, therefore, must equip future architects with PAMA design skill sets if ownership of prefabricated architecture is to have meaning, just as the introduction to computer-aided design in the 1970s became a vital tool for practising architects today.

Modular hotel building at Bristol Airport (UK) with bedroom suites on each side of a central corridor. (Photo by author)

Assembly or Construction?

Rethinking Building

We identify PAMA as a means for delivering complete buildings through OSM processes. We recognize immediately our terms of reference relate to manufacturing as opposed to construction in a conventional sense. Common to both conventional construction and OSM are the design and fabrication of materials into components and sub-assemblies. The nature and extent of construction forms a significant industry within the UK and plays a major role in nearly every project (Anderson and Anderson, 2007). Under the umbrella of OSM, then, we attach assembly as being fundamental to the manufacturing process as these two activities inter-connect, insofar as they are dependent upon one another in arriving at the completed volumetric or modularized entity. The completed volumetric components thus consist of all external and internal walls, floor and roof assemblies together with a total

fit-out of all the internal spaces (including complete fit-outs of kitchens and bathrooms) with all internal and external wall finishes and floor finishes, all of which are put together within the factory environment as one complete exercise. Delivering building projects in this way, therefore, where the superstructure is devoid of any connection with conventional construction activities on the site, save for the panelized installation process only, PAMA has a clear resonance with current thinking and future aspirations surrounding high-tech manufacturing. Community architecture should not be any different.

Professional Advice

As the OSM industry within the UK continues to gather greater momentum and with an ever-growing number of new participants entering the market as a consequence, there is also a growing element of confusion. Clients, building funders and procurement officials seek to understand with a greater clarity which part of the building might best be produced within the factory environment as an OSM and assembly process and which aspects are best executed in the conventional on-site construction process. For the uninitiated client or prospective building owner seeking to procure a single small-scale PAMA building (from a single house to an apartment block, a small community building or a set of classroom spaces up to a complete school building), there is always a challenge to get to grips with the numerous options available and the sub-division of activities surrounding the PAMA process, let alone the complexities associated with a building contract. Whilst such an adventure for the layperson is always best supported with the aid of the professional consultant, there is, however, the temptation for the brave individual to be persuaded by the off-site manufacturer's direct sales approach. Promotional and marketing materials for instant ready-made buildings available through internet shop windows can be very convincing to the inexperienced, with the potential for an unsatisfactory building as a result. As with any business transaction, dealing directly with a traditional builder or an off-site manufacturer can subject the inexperienced to exploitation at one end of the scale or potential financial ruin on the other and should be avoided.

The uninitiated can be easily exposed to technical jargon and be confused by its meaning and intent. Preferences sought by the individual client in terms of PAMA design options, materials, finishes, robustness, tests and certifications and the like can be managed to the client's disadvantage where there is a mind to do so. Similarly, the more experienced client, even one well versed in having delivered completed building projects through the more conventional route, might also question his or her ability to understand and fully appreciate precisely the differences between the familiar on-site construction route and those of the PAMA route. The more experienced client, however, will acknowledge the benefit of engaging with a professional consultant who is au fait in building procurement practices and procedures and less inclined to embark on a project where significant budgets might be under threat. Crucial to understanding PAMA and realizing the benefits to be achieved is the ability of the architect to identify at least the overlapping activities of PAMA with those relating to all of the on-site activities within the conventional construction process and not merely to view them in isolation from one another. In other words, he or she must understand the joint and separate interdependency and timing placed on the two separate disciplines coming together within the project delivery process. Given PAMA is a relatively new design discipline within various sectors with evolving forms of building contracts, there are design and construction professionals who have difficulty in differentiating the subtleties associated with PAMA as an alternative procurement route. There is a tendency to treat PAMA as merely another facet of conventional construction, which clearly is not the case.

PAMA Options Decisions

Under the auspices of prefabrication, factory assembly processes and on-site construction processes are often seen as being poles apart although the interrelationship between the two entities must be close in many ways for the project to be successful. Activities associated with constructing a building on the site are familiar to many, even if not in precise detail; at least a general understanding is within the grasp of most observers from beyond the site hoarding. We are used to seeing a construction site surrounded by protective hoarding within which there are large items of machinery with a small army of operatives busy at work. We eventually see a structure evolving from below ground in the form of foundations, then eventually the semblance of a superstructure either of concrete or steel framing, or, perhaps, in the case of smaller-scale construction projects, a traditional or conventional masonry build solution will eventually present itself, usually of brick and block construction. There are, of course, other forms of project procurement processes where each is dictated by the building's design use, the specific site context, project cost and its delivery date, to name but a few, and all of them make up the general ingredients of project delivery.

Project procurement by way of PAMA through OSM offers a viable alternative to conventional construction methods in a number of sectors and the differences which prevail between OSM and on-site activities are vast and significant. In many instances this relates directly to time and cost savings and central to achieving these is the ability to make early decisions. In essence, where full volumetric or modular solutions are the most viable option for the project, OSM provides the ability to produce in excess of 85–90 per cent of the completed building within the factory environment but not the full 100 per cent. Employing PAMA within a factory environment to remove up to 90 per cent of the normal on-site construction activities and associated costs is a significant feature of most project budgets. The remaining

10 per cent is then devoted to site preparation where the below-ground works (consisting of mainly services and foundations) will be installed. Whilst the first of the volumetric components are being assembled within the factory the main contractor is already preparing the site in readiness for the delivery of the completed volumetric/modular units. These two activities should be carried out in parallel so as to maximize the best use of time and to minimize the main contractor's time on-site, thereby reducing his/her preliminary costs to the project.

Other forms of volumetric or modular provision are also available from manufacturers who prefer to limit their involvement to producing only a shell and core type modular unit without any fit-out. This option is where the wall panels, floor cassettes and ceiling lids are assembled into a modular unit and delivered to the site for the main contractor to install first- and second-fix electrics and plumbing, all of the internal and external finishes and final fit-out on the construction site. This approach in many respects defeats the purpose of modular buildings as much of the time and cost benefits to be enjoyed by the PAMA route are not fully realized by the client but it is often preferred by the main contractor as much of the sub-contractor work packages and profit potential

would come under his/her remit as opposed to that of the manufacturer.

There is always an urgency for the project team to create time savings and recognizing more time spent by the main contractor on-site the greater potential exists for him to realize an increased profit potential through his own site preliminary costs. Equally, for the client, the reduction in time that the main contractor remains on-site is reflected in lower preliminary costs, together with the building being available to generate revenue at an earlier time than that offered by conventional construction. This is one specific aspect of project delivery where OSM processes demonstrate both a cost and time saving. The ability of the client and the professional team to comprehend manufacturing attributes and constraints at the project's initiation and strategic planning stage is fundamental to the success of the project and the client's aspirations and goals. Early decisions are key, therefore, for significant benefits: time and cost savings, consistent quality (where superior workmanship and precision are more easily achieved) and the ability of operatives to work in a single location in a safer all-weather environment; these benefits are indicative of the attributes associated with prefabricated architecture through PAMA manufacturing processes.

Precision, Exactness and Tolerances

Workmanship Standards

When we consider site conditions, we appreciate the nature of the place. The dynamics of the construction site comprise a multitude of events and activities, all at varying scales and levels of intensity, where the rough and tumble of large plant and machinery activities are mixed with the finesse needed for delivering good-quality architectural detailing and finishes. On-site tolerances can be specified from 2–3mm up to 20mm in certain instances whereas the precision and exactness within the OSM process is expected to

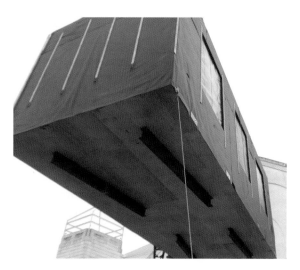

Modular classroom unit being delivered to the site for the contractor to complete the external cladding and internal fit-out on-site. (Courtesy of Structural Timber Products Ltd)

be achieved in the region of 1–2mm at most. Whilst tolerances within the on-site construction environment are well understood by the design and construction teams alike, overseeing quality control between the various trades and sub-contracting elements continues to be a high priority for the project team.

Workmanship standards and quality control are features of high focus for all on-site conventional construction projects and especially for the architect prior to issuing a Practical Completion Certificate, when the final inspection process can present last-minute problems which are usually associated with standards of workmanship. There is always an urgency from both the main contractor and the client funder, with the architect adjudicating on what is and is not acceptable quality. Debates surrounding

reasonable quality are usually where conflict may erupt. More serious and involved issues surrounding acceptable quality relating to conventional construction applications would usually be identified during the actual construction stages. Indeed, whilst acceptable standards of workmanship are usually identifiable and predictable there is always a potential for opinions to differ as to what is or is not acceptable unless samples have been provided from the outset.

A traditional form of contract provides some scope for the architect to prescribe and set down precisely what is required through the drawings and specification although the true intention and meaning can be brought into question by the construction team, where there is a mind to do so. A design and build contract, on the other hand, where much of the final design and materials come under the remit of the contractor, there is a huge potential for disagreement surrounding acceptable or expected workmanship and standards unless they are adequately and accurately provided for within the Employer's Requirements (ERs) at the time of tendering. Where professional opinions differ significantly on matters relating to standards of workmanship and quality of materials the potential for project delay can be serious for both the main contractor and the client funder, with overrun costs accumulating on a daily basis. Within the current conventional build environment the ability to predict a totally consistent quality result for every project is perhaps beyond reasonable expectations, especially when much of the workmanship is highly dependent upon the weather conditions, the skills, training and motivation of the construction teams, delivery dates and budget constraints together with other support activities involved at every level of the construction process. (*See also* Chapter 7.)

The primary consideration surrounding the factory assembly process is the ability to cater for precise measurement for on-site applications and to deliver this standard on a consistent basis. For a conventional build project, on-site conditions allow for specified tolerances depending on the materials and construction methods to be employed. This is not the

Precision external cladding in prefabricated building. (Courtesy of HOCA Practice)

Modular units in an assembly line production process. (Courtesy of CIMC MBS Ltd)

situation relating to the factory manufacturing processes, where tolerance expectations are far higher. The dependency and reliance on human endeavour to achieve consistent superior quality is always a huge expectation and can be a costly enterprise. For many building projects (housing and schools being prime examples), the quality assurance risk surrounding conventional build is now being substituted by more dependable options where the manufactured sub-assemblies and volumetric/modular components are more precision-made at the front end of the PAMA process and continue to remain a precision assembly process until the completed volumetric or modular unit is dispatched to the site for final assembly. For selected building projects automated machines and robotic intervention are becoming more significant players and are seen as means for delivering building projects in a more expeditious manner as well as eliminating the risk of poor workmanship. Manufacturing processes employ specific machinery and jigs that are purpose-designed to ensure the level of precision; exactness is achieved as a consistent norm. The factory assembly process can demonstrate its ability to deliver reliable results more easily than conventional build practices whilst at the same time offering the architect the confidence and design freedom to create working and living spaces which reflect current high workmanship standards and expectations.

Precision and Comparisons

Very few would challenge the manufacture of a motor car to be anything less than meticulous in its precision and exactness. Within the manufacturing plant the materials and sub-assemblies are on hand, just in time, at their respective locations on the assembly line in a precise and organized way to allow further human or robotic intervention to complete the assembly process of the entire vehicle. We recognize, too, the precision with which each of the components is assembled. Even the joint gaps between the various components forming the body are consistent, regular and meticulous in the manner in which they are consistently assembled in order to highlight their design as a feature. They are all the same and consistently fit together like a glove, one car after another driving off the assembly line as expected and meeting prescribed standards and specification at the completion of their assembly process. Beyond the average assembly line for an average motor car, some cars are of a particular high brand and prestige. Their

manufacturers, of course, will aspire to such superior quality materials that their interiors alone are deemed to be masterpieces in craftsmanship where attention to detail is paramount and precision is a byword for the norm; that is, end-to-end design and manufacture exist as one compete entity. We identify the car as being a good example of precision engineering by the way it is conceived from the outset with all of the detail design and manufacturing processes developed as one joined-up exercise before the finished product is presented to the market. Indeed, the motor manufacturing industry worldwide 'provide[s] insight into how tighter integration with contractors might evolve' (McKinsey, 2017).

To what extent could one sensibly compare the building of a house, school, hospital or indeed any community building with building a motor car? What single feature should we reasonably assume to be similar if not the same? It would, of course, be less than reasonable to compare the manufacture of a prestigious motor car with the activities associated with a conventional construction project on an exposed site. In the first instance, motor car production is founded on a manufacturing process which remains at one location with a static workforce always in the correct work position where the efficiencies of

Precision manufacturing and assembly associated with the motor manufacturing industry have set standards in quality now expected for prefabricated and modular architecture. (Photo by author)

Precision internal fit-out quality from manufacturing and assembly processes is now being sought as standard for prefabricated and modular architecture. (Photo by author)

Robotic car production in a modern assembly plant.

the assembly line is best served. On-site construction activities, on the other hand, might be identified as nomadic as one building project is completed on one site, so the entire construction team with their plant machinery, equipment and workforce must relocate once again to the next site location.

The capacity, therefore, for achieving consistently high levels of precision and accuracy for each individual conventional construction project is disadvantaged significantly by not being able to accommodate repetition of assembly from one project to the next of the established, fully functioning assembly line which is tried and tested for greater efficiency and standards. Comparing on-site construction processes with those associated with PAMA factory manufacturing is very simple in as much as the two disciplines consist of a different mindset, starting at the initial design concept stage. The ability for building projects in the UK to deliver some semblance of parity in terms of consistency, cost and quality assurance with that of the motor manufacturing industry has not arrived yet. However, current thinking appears to indicate a new mood of expectation where high-performance machine automation and robotic assembly, even

Plant and machinery being transferred to the next site for a typical conventional construction project. (Photo by author)

robotic design through machine learning, will become instrumental in manufacturing buildings as opposed to constructing them in the conventional way.

The PAMA philosophy already exists outside the UK, as in Japan, where the Toyota Housing Corporation seeks to deliver housing projects founded on the principles derived from its motor manufacturing and assembly line skills and practices. For the UK, there is sufficient evidence to indicate that where elements of the existing construction process are substituted by ones designed under the auspices of PAMA as a prerequisite, it would be deemed to be an excellent first step. Extending the PAMA concept to the ultimate would suggest that even greater efficiencies and effectiveness are achieved where hand-built activities associated with conventional construction, especially in relation to the superstructure, are substituted by componentization and assembly processes from within the factory (Ung, 2018) but also by a greater utilization of artificial intelligence in assembly processes.

Component Assembly and Performance

Materials, Components and Assemblies

Central to every building project are the initial materials which produce components that create sub-assemblies and finally complete assemblies such as wall panels or completed modular units which are totally fitted out. Completed entities such as these are connected together, thus ultimately generating the building's superstructure as a total assembly or the 'whole', all elements of which perform a unique function in providing structural performance, fire protection, thermal performance, external finishes and cladding materials and so on. In his 'Three Tiers of Prefabrication' (2018), Ung identifies specific entities within prefabricated architecture where individual parts, components and assemblies are brought together to create completed buildings.

A completed window, for example, would be classified as a component part of a building, which itself consists of a series of materials which are processed and fabricated into the final window component for the building. The very essence of the window will consist of a number of primary materials and components, usually of a metal or timber along with other supporting materials, so as to produce a complete window entity or component. Clearly, a window unit of this nature could not be sensibly fabricated on the construction site given the very high level of precision and quality control that is vital to meet current window technology and standards. Fabricating components of this nature can only sensibly be achieved within a factory-controlled environment which allows for suitable testing to be undertaken to satisfy performance requirements.

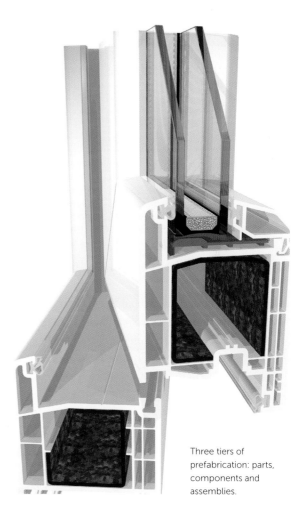

Three tiers of prefabrication: parts, components and assemblies.

Precision window installation for a modular building at Bristol, UK. (Photo by author)

window. Consequently, the finished window as a completed product has a history: from a collection of raw materials to individual parts and small components assembled into a number of sub-assemblies which, when combined and put through the manufacturing process, arrive ultimately as a completed assemblage, the window unit. This end-to-end design and manufacturing process represents the very essence employed for specific buildings adopting the PAMA ethos. Within the make-up of any building, then, whether it is a single house or a multi-storey commercial building, conventional construction or PAMA build, there are always many hundreds, if not thousands, of different entities used. Conventional construction processes relate to assembling materials and sub-assemblies on the site as an on-site construction process, as opposed to PAMA manufacturing and assembly processes where the assembly is undertaken and completed within a controlled factory environment and then delivered to the site for installation either as a panelized system or as a final assemblage in the case of modular units. There is scope, therefore, for recognizing a clear distinction between on-site construction and factory-produced modular buildings where completed volumetric modular units are 'assembled' at the site location to create the whole modular building.

If one closely examines the actual make-up of the window unit it will be observed that numerous individual parts and components are required for its ultimate assembly. The hinges, for instance, are components which are probably manufactured in a totally different factory specializing in manufacturing just that type of component which, again, is fabricated from materials and individual parts. Equally, the window locks and security systems would possibly be procured from a specialist source as, indeed, is the glass for the double glazing. But it goes beyond this: the actual metal, the very core material of the window unit, arrives at the factory as either flat sheet or preformed to the required extrusion to suit the functional requirements and design for the

Geometry in Design

Ready-made manufactured buildings with their familiar standardized modular units (as opposed to an architect design modular solution) are plentiful. Examples of such 'helicopter jobs' are familiar sights throughout the UK and what was intended initially to function only as a temporary solution has often remained in place for many decades. Whilst their presence has served to reinforce commonly held perceptions surrounding 'prefab' as a visual blight on the landscape or an ugly statement provoking horror with a streetscape, they have nonetheless demonstrated a robustness in having lasted for such a long period.

Modular building providing a ubiquitous temporary accommodation solution. (Photo by author)

By contrast, the degree to which prefabricated modular units now adhere to current building standards and codes is due largely to the evolving technology which exploits the attributes of familiar building materials applied for a new use in PAMA buildings. Materials themselves have the capacity to be expressed as an integral part of the modular unit. Equally, manufactured components function not only as structural elements; they are also integral to the building's architecture. The joints between components, too, form a significant contribution to the building's aesthetic, as are the design gaps between the panels of a car. The size and proportions of the volumetric modular unit can provide a substantial presence in the architectural design solution by the manner in which they control scale and geometry when assembled together as the whole building. Salingaros (2008, p. 231) connects scale to sizes as reflecting human relevance: 'Structural order is a phenomenon that obeys its own laws. It connects built structure with visual structure on the human scale'. Leopold (2006) refers to the connection between architectural design and harmony as being a fundamental ingredient for all sciences and creations. The nature and size of components and completed assemblies expressed as a feature of, or within, the architectural design solution is representative of the architect's ability to capitalize fully by designing within manufacture and assembly (DfMA) ethos and, at the same time, embrace the surrounding characteristics of the site context. Where the architect is equipped with these design attributes, architectural design solutions under the auspices of PAMA can be realized in a humanized manner where scale and massing will evolve with a greater sense of meaning and appreciation.

Architectural Language

Client funders, together with their design teams, seeking a viable alternative to the conventional procurement route must be satisfied by PAMA's capacity to deliver structural spans and robustness together with exploiting design options for employing existing or new materials in an innovative way, as a new science. Considering the architectural elements for a PAMA project, preferably at the strategic stage but certainly at the initial design concept stage, has to be a prerequisite if the full benefits of PAMA are to be realized by clients and funders. The design discipline that surrounds successful PAMA buildings will have a capacity to recognize components and sub-assemblies as architectural elements integral for realizing the building's architecture in the first instance but equally its final massing in relation to the expressing modular components or sub-assemblies.

The primary emphasis for PAMA project success is represented by a design strategy where the larger the modular unit that can be delivered to the site

Modular architectural design defining an architectural language in style: building under assembly.

Finished building displaying its unique character.

for assembly, the greater the realization of quality maintenance and time- and cost-efficiencies. Further, it would be reasonable to indicate that the actual architecture of the building can be more clearly expressed by its components and/or the totality of the building's complete modular assemblage, should this design decision form part of the design intent at concept design stage. In other words, the architectural language for the building can be expressed or aspects of the building's design can be highlighted by the design for these two entities, either singularly or collectively, and where spatial organization can also be defined as part of this mix. Salingaros (2008, p. 231) describes language as the forerunner

for style: 'A form of language governs the built form in all its expressions: geometry, composition, structure, materials, surfaces, etc.' He goes on to suggest that, in essence, we refer to it as 'architectural style'. As new PAMA technologies, automation, robotics, artificial intelligence and innovative assembly processes emerge, which truly perform the purpose for which they are intended, so too will prefabricated architecture emerge as a distinct architectural style embracing unique and distinct design features and characteristics that become synonymous with PAMA as a design discipline in its own right whilst, at the same time, currently held 'prefab' perceptions will be dispelled.

Manufacture and Assembly Processes

Adopting New Thinking

Whilst recognizing the distinct differences that exist between conventional build and PAMA, there is nonetheless a belief within certain quarters that architectural design principles applied to conventional construction initially can be automatically transferred to OSM and assembly as a seamless process. The difficulty with this thinking, however, is that these procurement routes are totally different, necessitating totally different approaches from the very beginning of a project, starting at concept design stage. The conventional build route might be an immediate choice at the project strategic stage primarily due to the design and construction teams' familiarity with traditional build skills, practices and procedures. Indeed, the nature and extent of options available through conventional build are perceived as endless, as indeed they are where an endless budget is available to match. Current research and UK government thinking, on the other hand, highlight the fact that

if the UK is to have a realistic chance of meeting its housing, schools and hospitals building programmes to realistic budgets, the construction industry needs to convert much of the existing on-site construction activities to OSM and assembly processes (House of Lords Report, 2017–19). Fundamental to achieving the House of Lords objective, then, is the necessity for design and construction professionals to embrace PAMA ethos as integral to the project delivery process, and as a first-choice option. The alternative would be for more off-site manufacturers to engage directly with clients in the end-to-end project delivery but recognizing, too, the importance of adopting and incorporating competent architectural design in parallel with fabrication design as well as all associated site works, which is not the preference of most off-site manufacturers.

DfMA

Within the manufacturing and assembly environment the core ingredients necessary to deliver an

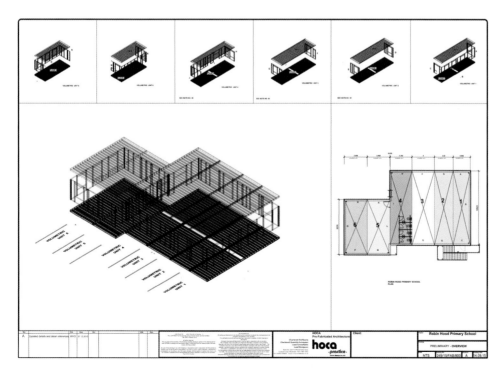

Prefabricated modular design: this strategic planning stage is the optimum time for maximizing cost benefit. (Courtesy of HOCA Practice)

end-to-end component or product consist of a collection of selected materials brought together by a sequence of manufacturing and assembly processes. A key ingredient for the successful delivery of a PAMA building project is the ability of the architect at the initiation stage to deliver the design which embraces all aspects connected with the manufacturing and assembly as an all-inclusive design. It is crucial for the architect to have a full working knowledge and understanding of components and assemblies associated with the building. This might be the assembly process for a wall panel component for a panelized construction project or the full assembly for a volumetric modular unit consisting of all external and internal walls together with the floor and lid assemblies. In order to design out the 'disconnect' that currently exists between architectural design and fabrication design the obvious must happen: when the architectural design incorporates the design for manufacture and assembly (DfMA) as a combined design discipline the project will always produce a superior result.

Current PAMA design practice demonstrates that where the architectural concept design includes fabrication design in parallel as a total holistic design strategy, the final architectural detail design responds accordingly. With architectural design embracing a sound knowledge of component design and the manner in which they are assembled in the fabrication process, a properly well-coordinated project is formed which represents a fully integrated end-to-end design process. Moreover, the project is spared the constant design revisions and changes that are often too frequent through misunderstanding or unrealistic expectations of both the architect and the manufacturer where zones of design responsibility and aspects of detailing are the issue. Errors and defects, too, can be easily detected during each of the combined design stages and ultimately during the assembly process, should they ever reach that stage.

The model result is for the building to be handed over at completion (RIBA Work Stage 6 – Practical Completion) with zero defects. Whilst this might prove to be an idealistic objective for conventional build it is less so with PAMA, especially when the building's design is initiated to incorporate design for manufacture (DFM) and design for assembly (DFA) principles as a prerequisite for the total design solution. Historically, we associate DFM and DFA with products and assemblies to be employed more as stand-alone elements or as an assembly of materials and components which make up familiar volumetric component products; that is, they are considered to be something more akin to the parts that would go into manufacturing an engine or a vacuum cleaner. Equally, there are a vast number of elements required for the construction of a building on-site where materials, individual parts, components and sub-assemblies, ranging from a door hinge to a completed stair installation, are assembled within the factory environment and transported to the site for their final installation into the building.

Prefabricated architecture now brings a new dimension to the process, as external and internal walls, floors and roofs, as well as complete internal fit-outs of all the internal spaces, can be realized from within the factory. Indeed, the scope of the actual site 'construction' for the superstructure is transformed to become more of a site 'assembly process' where completed volumetric modular units are transported from the factory to the site location and constitute the vast majority of the building's procurement. Delivering totally fitted-out modular units is demonstrating itself to be a very viable alternative to on-site construction. Regretfully, the missing link to date is the absence of the architect's end-to-end design input to the manufacturing and assembly process where currently much of the architectural design comes under the influence of the manufacturer alone.

Taking Design Ownership

By architects becoming more design-savvy as to the composition of various materials that make up wall and floor sub-assemblies and by exploiting the manner in which the various components perform, they impose their direct influence on the overall architectural design solution. Until recently sub-assemblies and modular units were considered to be outside the remit of the architect's brief and often identified as a 'contractor design portion' which ultimately is left with the selected manufacturer. A more recent urgency for procuring buildings through PAMA, however, has caused a change in this thinking, where the composition, size and performance capabilities of components, sub-assemblies and modular units are fast becoming relevant to the total architectural design solutions. Clearly, by considering the detail design of the actual completed assemblies (modular units) and their component and sub-assembly within, PAMA as a natural part of the final design solution represents a total three-dimensional approach to prefabricated architecture design.

If architects are to take ownership of the total design process, as opposed to accepting certain limitations and restrictions imposed by particular factory systems and solutions available from manufacturers, they must not only acquaint themselves with the buildings' components and their sub-assemblies but also possess a good understanding of the manufacturing processes relating to the same. This will include the architect taking cognisance of the site context, its restrictions for access, main and local road widths, and bridge widths and heights between the factory to the site, all of which will inform the final design solution at concept design stage by the size of the volumetric/modular units that can be delivered to the site. (*See also* Chapter 7.) Architects seeking to develop a design specialism in prefabricated architecture need to recognize a change in mindset is necessary and behind this lies the prospect of taking ownership of the factory entity as being integral to the overall design solution for a given site. Architects designing different prefabricated buildings and specifying their various component parts, even with repeated use, will transform current practice and promote prefabricated architecture as a recognized design discipline in its own right.

Chapter Four

Standardization and Prefabricated Solutions

Introduction

When Edward I embarked upon building Harlech Castle in 1282 it would be reasonable to presume no consideration was applied to standardization as we would relate to it today. All construction work had to be hand-built with an acceptance that building materials tended to be of stone for the load-bearing walls, several metres thick in some places and twelve metres high, with timber for floors and roof. Designed by architect James of St George, who was influenced by castle design in other parts of Europe, Harlech Castle was a stunning feat of engineering for its time, built without the assistance of mechanization and technology we associate with today. Standardization had to wait a further six hundred years for the Industrial Revolution to arrive to cast its influence, which diverted building practices and techniques from wholly trade crafts to machine production; trade craft ever since has remained subservient to the might of mass production and standardization. Increased use of machine production and factory-made prefabricated components in current building projects has never waned since, which merely highlights a preference to reduce labour-intensive trade crafts, either because of a desire for greater efficiency or perhaps seeking to substitute for the diminishing quality in trade crafts, or both.

Harlech Castle, Gwynedd, North Wales: load-bearing construction 1282–89. (Photo by author)

Standardization is limited and restricted to the capacity and capabilities of the machines and technology that exist for the production of a given component and the final end product. Within the constraints of these limitations, however, the potential to cope with most component and assembly requirements as envisaged today already exists. Where architects seek to create new prefabricated and modular architecture, so too will the requirement for new materials and component design emerge, which, for now, can only be considered and designed in relation to the capabilities of the machinery available. (*See* Chapter 2's section headed 'Design: the Science and Technology Aesthetic'.) The alternative would be for machinery and its technology to evolve and innovate prefabrication design in parallel with, but preferably in advance of, emerging product design and innovation, which would suggest machine designers and engineers are ahead in the design race. (*See* Chapter 3 under the heading 'Precision and Comparisons'.) This approach is realistically more viable where sufficient multi-production, but preferably mass production, transpires as opposed to a single one-off designed project.

William Morris (1834–96) is notable in British culture as the pioneer of the Arts and Crafts movement; architecture was his first experience within the arts. He aspired to the concept of the single house and decried the use of machinery of any description in the creation of art. Thus, for Morris, machinery, the factory and notions of mass production are therefore incapable of producing art. However, within the sphere of prefabricated architecture currently, the architect's design solutions are a direct result of and dependent upon the input, capacity and capabilities of machinery and its technology, irrespective of whether manufactured components are for a single house, a large housing project or a large public building. The art of architecture, then, might be attributed to the extent of the machine's capabilities or, more especially perhaps, the ingenuity of the architect

Stone cottage circa 1800s. (Photo by author)

Stone lintel. (Photo by author)

and his/her ability to extract innovative design and aesthetic beauty from machinery; this latter might be the catalyst in the first instance. As a dedicated socialist and medievalist Morris was appalled by the advances in evolving mechanization and concepts embracing mass production, seeking instead to extol values and practices associated with simple design and traditional craftsmanship. In the context of the Industrial Revolution, which Morris was born into, he was seen as a total rebel by the evolving leaders of British industry and invention. His terms of reference to the arts and the period of patronage preceding the Industrial Revolution (which was as far as he was prepared to advance his capacity in his ability to recognize an evolving modern world) is perhaps something akin to the present Prince of Wales in some of the latter's references to modern architecture.

In business, however, standardization and mass production are compelling partners as together they offer the most fitting combination for capitalizing on concepts surrounding repetitive mass production in the first instance. Economies of scale, being the primary feature in any enterprise set up for standardized production, dictate the actual viability and commercial realism and success of the product and of the business ultimately. Being able to exploit mass production on every possible level is paramount to sustaining a business entity, especially in relation to prefabrication, and equates with claims of many manufacturers that government departments are failing to commit to volume in their attempts to solve the current housing shortages. Volume might also be explained by reference to the larger container ship: the more containers it can carry the greater the ability of the shipping company to provide a keener price per container shipped. Hence, the urgency within the shipping industry to build the super-container ship is apparent.

In order for standardized prefabrication technology to be explored to the fullest it is incumbent upon architects, especially, to grasp opportunities that now exist. Architects have a responsibility for rethinking the art of architectural design in parallel with the vast potential that standardized prefabrication has to offer as a design principle, and particularly in times of acute financial restraint. More especially, architects must examine the essence of modular manufacturing and assembly processes in parallel with modular design processes, bespoke design and even innovative system design methodologies, where inevitably a specific, recognizable and identifiable entity for defining prefabricated and modular architecture will emerge.

Manufacturing Technology and Design

The area where technology can have a true influence in prefabrication and achieve the greatest aesthetic

Prefabricated timber-framed building, with laminated timber beams, columns and connections creating the architectural aesthetic and the structural engineering as a joined-up design solution. (Courtesy of HOCA Practice)

Lloyds building, London, expressing the building external envelope.

Architecture and engineering: laminated timber columns and beam with metal connections form the main structural support for the building. (Photo by author)

impact is where the elements of connection forming part of the structure are expressed as part of the overall architecture of the building. For example, the structural elements employed to maintain the structural integrity of the building when expressed as a design element thereby form an influential aspect of the building's architecture and its aesthetic. In cases such as this, one could reasonably maintain that the building's structural engineering embraces the architectural design or that it becomes the architectural design.

Aspects surrounding building services engineering can also contribute in a similar manner as the structural engineering. Typical examples of this are the Lloyd's building in London (UK) and the Pompidou Centre in Paris (France) where the building services expressed externally by design form part of the building's external envelope. Here the architecture consists of not just the glass façade but more especially of the lifts, service ducts and features displaying the building's circulation. Consequently, the Lloyd's building is not intended to be considered as a series of

separate components and elements but as a total and whole architectural composition. The entire visual experience, therefore, consists of balance and order but at the same time a fair helping of unpredictability, as one expects from Mozart's treatment of music.

Evolving Technology

Prefabrication, however, is not a feature that just happened by default. There is a purpose which initially has a bearing on demand and efficiency, usually relating to time and cost and the viability of the project, all of which are influenced in turn by the advances in manufacturing technology. When examining the nature and extent of building requirements it soon becomes very evident that the application of science to production revolves around technology. Technology embodies almost every facet imaginable, from tools to machines and processes, materials to component products and, of course, design information which functions as a catalyst for deciding which

Automated butterfly turning table for panel production. (Courtesy of Frame Homes (SW) Ltd)

Factory fit-out creating high-quality finishes. (Photo by author)

of these ingredients are employed and how best they might perform their designated function.

So where within the architectural design process will prefabrication impose a measure of influence? The scope of design possibilities within the sphere of prefabrication can be endless, with even greater design opportunities evolving rapidly. Irrespective of whether prefabricated buildings are designed through panelization or modularization, one limitation is the length of the truck delivering prefabricated elements to the construction site; this remains a common denominator. Therein lies a design discipline

associated with the manufacturing process and, because of this, the actual design and installation process for the building is influenced accordingly.

Attitudes, Perceptions and Economics

Distinct differences of views exist between architects and building funders, who possess aspirations for either prefabricated panelized or modular buildings and design, and the industrialists, who are in the business of producing modular components and buildings

Prefabricated temporary classrooms, Surrey. (Photo by author)

in the most economic fashion and are generally devoid of any particular architectural design philosophies. Architects on the one hand would envisage employing modular systems with their standardized attributes as a means for producing pragmatic building solutions but, at the same time, endeavour to realize a design solution founded on aspirations relating to architectural principles. Smith (2010 p. 159) stated: 'Modular architecture is often associated with utopian ideals of the 1960s in which architects developed proposals that were temporary, mobile, and used new materials and techniques of erection and disassembly.' This is not necessarily the approach being sought in today's context where a prerequisite is the ability to produce prefabricated buildings expected to have a life span of not less than sixty years and supported with warranties. The industrialist, too, would have an equally valid goal but not necessarily one which is akin to architectural design principles as a fundamental basis. Common practice in manufacture concentrates more on the marketability of any given product and standardized prefabricated modular buildings are no exception. The thrust that lies behind most ready-made modular design systems today is to bring cost-effectiveness, shorter construction time and greater efficiency to

the client or client funder, where buildings have more permanency as opposed to that of past decades where prefabricated buildings were seen as a means of fixing an immediate shortage, whether housing, schools or medical centres and the like.

Structural Grid and PAMA

There will always be a requirement for structure in a building. It is the structural elements which make the building stand up and remain in place. Prior to the Industrial Revolution most buildings in the UK consisted of masonry often referred to as 'traditional' or 'conventional' build. For example, conventional build practice where traditional building materials were used to provide the wall structure is referred to as producing a load-bearing structure, as in a stone cottage or a brick-built house. The same materials also provide the means with which to form the external wall enclosure for the building and the internal partition walls to create internal spaces. Load-bearing wall elements are used to carry the internal floors and the roof. Traditional load-bearing buildings such as the grand houses of the past, many with a clearly defined symmetry, certainly had a plan layout arrangement where a similarity in room spaces and size prevails but without being subjected to the rigid discipline of a structural grid system as employed in building projects today by which the building is set out. Whilst a sense of design freedom might appear to have existed in positioning walls at will, thereby allowing the architect to exploit opportunities for creating a totally bespoke creation, it is (however) more of a myth than reality, as design limitations and restrictions were reflected by the capacity, capability and limitations of the traditional materials used at the time. Common sense too dictated that a more structurally stable solution would result where one wall was placed on top of another. For modern architects, design freedom prevails within most community architecture and housing projects where small structural spans and load-bearing requirements can be accommodated within conventional build practices, but the laws of physics still exist in relation to their construction. Beyond the more usual domestic-scale projects where larger spaces and structural spans are required, employing a grid

system is integral to managing the building's design where generating greater structural efficiency economic pragmatism is a prerequisite.

The grid is a well-established vehicle used by architects to determine internal space arrangements along with a building's external form; ideally, both these elements should correspond with an economic span arrangement for the structural frame. Grid lines in buildings are also used by structural engineers as a tool for positioning and calculating sizes of columns and beams, whether concrete, steel or timber, forming the structure of the building to the architect's design. To appreciate the value of the grid in the building's design it is necessary to accept the grid idea as a means for defining design rules around which the architectural geometry of the prefabricated building's concept design and space arrangement is realized.

The grid does not have to be so rigid and inflexible as to deprive the architect of design expression, as within the main set of grids a set of sub-grids can be introduced into the design. Specific internal space arrangements can be accommodated for a specific

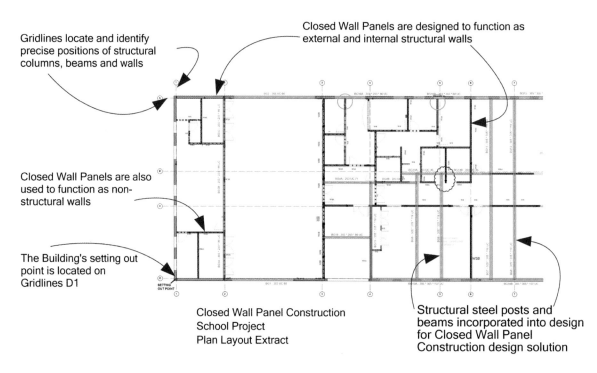

Gridlines locate and identify precise positions of structural columns, beams and walls

Closed Wall Panels are designed to function as external and internal structural walls

Closed Wall Panels are also used to function as non-structural walls

The Building's setting out point is located on Gridlines D1

Closed Wall Panel Construction
School Project
Plan Layout Extract

Structural steel posts and beams incorporated into design for Closed Wall Panel Construction design solution

Structural grid arrangement. (Diagram courtesy of HOCA Practice)

aesthetic without sabotaging the integrity of design rules determined by the grid's geometry. Architectural form and language, too, can be determined by how the structural frame of the building is expressed as a main element within which a subdivision of a smaller modularity exists. Alternatively, the architect may choose to treat the building elevations by ignoring the structural grid altogether and opt for expressing a different modularity to accommodate the external cladding or glazing panels to create a more enhanced aesthetic or as the most economical solution, or both.

Prefabricated and modular architecture is no different in how it adopts the rules of the grid geometry. There is, however, one certain criterion in grid spacing and that is transportation. This one factor forms the primary influence in designing for PAMA irrespective of whether the building is designed for panelized construction or volumetric modular. Panel sizes or the size of the volumetric modular unit or module are governed by the capacity of the roads, the clear height under any bridges along the route from the factory to the site location and the preferred delivery vehicle width for cost-efficiencies. The manner in which structural grids are used in relation to panelized construction, as opposed to a modular build project, is different. With panelized construction the size of the panels does not necessarily relate to the structural grid for the building, as they are manufactured to accommodate a design for a conventional build regime where the structural grid has a greater relationship to the structural frame and not the walls created by the prefabricated system for the building.

For modular designed buildings the opposite is the case, however, as each volumetric modular unit or module directly influences and dictates the actual plan layout arrangement of the final building. This is because the total building grid is established from the size of the modular unit itself and set out accordingly. The size of the modular unit or module derives from the concept design which ultimately drives and thereby determines the size of the grid, both horizontally and vertically, so as to accommodate the

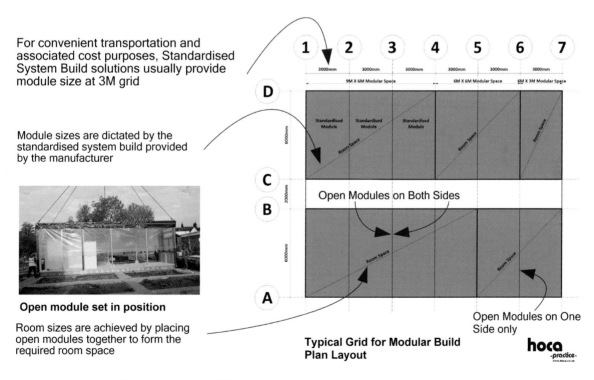

For convenient transportation and associated cost purposes, Standardised System Build solutions usually provide module size at 3M grid

Module sizes are dictated by the standardised system build provided by the manufacturer

Open module set in position

Room sizes are achieved by placing open modules together to form the required room space

Typical Grid for Modular Build Plan Layout

hoca ·practice·

Typical grid arrangement. (Diagram courtesy of HOCA Practice, photo by author)

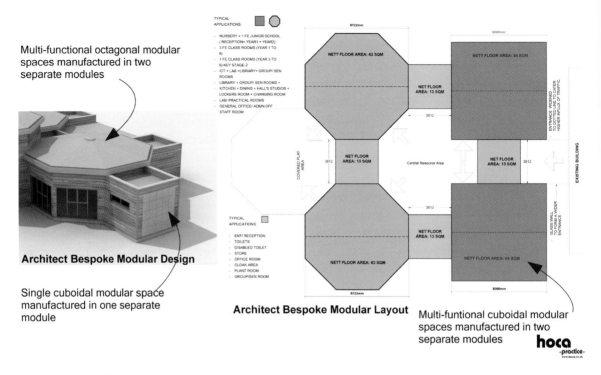

Multi-functional octagonal modular spaces manufactured in two separate modules

Architect Bespoke Modular Design

Single cuboidal modular space manufactured in one separate module

Architect Bespoke Modular Layout

Multi-funtional cuboidal modular spaces manufactured in two separate modules

Architect design grid for bespoke modular projects. (Diagram and photo courtesy of HOCA Practice)

most efficient plan layout arrangement. Defining the structural grid to satisfy the preferred plan layout arrangement will also be reflected in the elevations for the building. The gridlines for the building's setting out, therefore, will in turn influence the visual appearance of the building. The design skill of the architect is brought to bear as a consequence by the manner in which s/he decides to manage the connections, junctions, materials and architectural detailing for the prefabricated and modular design solution.

Customization

The thrust that lies behind prefabrication is its connection with standardization and its association with mass-produced components and products. The epitome of standardization was introduced by Henry Ford when in 1910 he established the first assembly line for reducing the production time for the Model T. All cars were the same standardized product, repeated and consistent. The emphasis placed on

standardization in housing, too, relates to the housing shortages that began in the early part of the twentieth century and consisted of using particular products from a small number of manufacturing industrialists. Given the urgency surrounding housing, little if any consideration was given by individual industrialists to providing some variety in their unitized housing system and a 'one type fits all' philosophy was applied accordingly. Consequently, the only variation that existed at the time was that resulting from the minor differences between manufacturers.

The current housing sector, together with other sectors, is less tolerant of a restricted standardized approach, whether it is housing, schools, sports and recreation, healthcare or comparable community architecture projects. There is a demand for individualism and for each building or project to express its own personality and character; in former years this would have been associated with a traditional bespoke design approach under the direction of an architect, something more akin to William Morris's ideal perhaps. In order for prefabricated and modular architecture to announce its presence in a creative design environment and justify its existence, it too must be capable of delivering design excellence, flexibility and superior build quality as a prerequisite. Customization can mean different things to different people and situations but, in reality, it represents a modification or adjustment in some way. Customization in relation to panelization, for instance, may represent the ability to create specific wall panel lengths and heights to suit a particular project for on-site construction applications. Modular build, too, can be customized to provide various widths and lengths of the modular unit or module. Whilst seeking to accommodate specific requirements and preferences for a particular design or individual client, both, however, must maintain their respective manufacturing processes if their pricing strategy is to remain competitive.

Customization is also seen by some manufacturing industrialists as a means for satisfying an emerging market where customer needs, preference, personality and character are recognized as essential ingredients in the mix for their unique building or project. For some manufacturers, however, this is approached at a superficial level necessitating only the absolute minimum of adjustment and without any physical change to their already established tried and tested system build solution. Indeed, why should it, if it means a total change to their system and manufacturing and assembly processes? It is, however, used as a tool by various manufacturers to attract interest to their specific building system and to seek to personalize a solution for a particular situation. Good salesmanship can demonstrate to the less informed client how easily a manufacturer can automatically

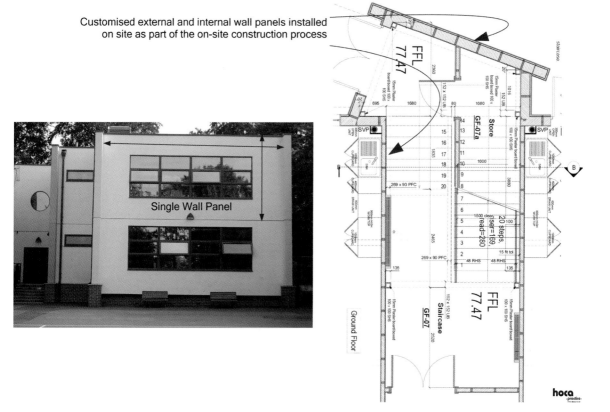

Customized full storey height wall panels designed and manufactured to incorporate doors and windows as one entity. (Diagram courtesy of HOCA Practice, photo by author)

customize their prefabrication method to accommodate specific preferences in an attempt to highlight how preferable their system would be over a competitor. This, alas, is rarely the case without implications arising during the on-site installation process and especially with panelization. The final build usually demonstrates the limitations of the standardized/unitized system build product; this may not be apparent perhaps until much later in the installation process when there is little if any opportunity to take corrective measures without incurring significant costs and time delay. With modular building the modular unit or module originates from a jig from which all the walls, floor and lid can be controlled to ensure more exacting tolerances, thereby creating repeat consistency for each modular unit and more assured installation.

For other manufacturers customization represents a totally different philosophy: they have the capabilities of taking an architect's concept design and delivering the building as a prefabricated architecture solution under a design and build contract, albeit adjusted somewhat to accommodate manufacturing, assembly and materials offered by the manufacturer for the building. A conventional construction project delivered using a design and build contract also has the propensity to deliver a building somewhat different in certain respects from the architect's concept intent. Client aspirations may not be fully realized as originally envisaged from the architect's original concept design, particularly in relation to architectural detailing and sometimes materials and finishes, as flexibility and options available may have to be adjusted, curtailed and even designed out by the manufacturer or contractor to reflect the budget available. Much of the disappointment, however, is often the result of a restricted budget from the outset and very often an impossible budget at that. Clients especially must recognize there is much more to a building project than what is seen above ground level and that consequently it is not possible to achieve a £300,000 project for £175,000 or a £3m project for £2m.

Customized Panelization

Customization can also be taken to the next level, where the architect's concept design is dedicated to delivering a bespoke prefabricated architecture design solution; that is, a one-off design. Within the current UK marketplace there are some reputable companies who have the ability to provide such bespoke prefabricated buildings as a specialism. This is not to be confused with a customized standard system build or unitized building as referred to earlier, where making only some minor adjustments to a ready-made standardized system is envisaged. Sourcing a prefabricated customized building from a manufacturer as a bespoke design is not common and is an endeavour where the architect needs to know and understand the preferred manufacturer's processes and capabilities. Even within this environment manufacturers will also have their preferred systems and specialisms, materials, manufacturing and installation processes, each offering options ranging through closed panel system, open panel system, structural insulated panel system (SIPS) or similar wall panel systems but in the UK they are rarely concrete panels (*see* Chapter 5, under the heading 'Precast Concrete Panels).

The final choice may consist of specialized timber engineering solutions or a mix of panelization and laminated timber beams and columns or panelization with steel posts and beams. Customized panelization units such as these are essentially wall panels and components manufactured in the factory to a predetermined size and specification to perform a given function and delivered to the site for installation as a conventional construction process. They are of such a nature as to be able to accommodate bespoke design objectives of the architect where flexible floor plan layouts and the ability to adhere to specific spaces or sizes are essential. Bespoke prefabricated panelization then comprises parts and components manufactured in a factory usually as timber engineering, rarely fabricated steel, and installed into the building as part of the overall building process. That is, they tend to form part of the on-site construction process delivered in a

Bespoke design facilitated with structural insulated panels (SIPs). (Photo by author)

components and sub-assemblies to create a completed modular unit or module. Each modular unit can consist of a single space or a number of spaces within a single module or a number of modules when joined (assembled) together to form a completed room or working space. The overall size and internal arrangement of the module tends to be less restricted when compared to predetermined modular system build with limitations inflicted by rigid standardization and unitization. The current market is now more focused and geared up to provide the level of flexibility expected, but within the limitations of the overall size of the modularized unit dictated by transportation. Consequently, in this instance also, customization is not necessarily introducing over-demanding requirements that would generate significant cost to the project. In fact, it would be reasonable to suggest the ability to dictate the actual size of the module required exists from the start of the concept design stage which generates the design criteria for the completed modular building or project. The architect should remain mindful, however, that the module size is restricted by the delivery vehicle being able to negotiate the roads designated for transporting from the factory to the site.

conventional way through a main contractor on-site and not in the context of prefabricated modular architecture delivered by a manufacturer as defined earlier. In some design and build projects it is known for the prefabricated architectural elements, forming part of the architect's concept design, to be substituted by tendering contractors seeking to offer an attractive alternative. This is something more akin to conventional build practices which the tendering contractors are more familiar with. It can be a ploy in order to direct profit margins away from the specialist manufacturer and towards the main contractors who are more familiar with the conventional build approach but does not necessarily mean cost savings for the client.

Open sided modular units brought together on site to form large open spaces as required

Customized Volumetric Modular

Modular building as commonly referred to today constitutes the assembly of prefabricated parts,

Steel-framed modular units up to 16m long, with internal space customized to architect's design. (Courtesy of HOCA Practice)

Irrespective of whether the project consists of panelized construction or modular build, customization is somewhat of a misnomer in that it does not need to apply to prefabricated architecture in the current spheres of panel component manufacture and of modular manufacture and assembly. Design rules, flexibility, restrictions and limitations are adhered to in relation to factory manufacturing and delivery constraints. Customization therefore has no myth nor mystery attached to it. It forms a natural part of the prefabricated architecture design process as a new building science from the start which begins with the concept design stage, and in the capable hands of a skilled architect will be managed accordingly.

Standardized Components and System Build

Standardized Components

Within the sphere of prefabricated architecture, the assumption is that standardization is integral to the process. Indeed, current thinking revolves around the expectation that economies and efficiencies in the manufacturing process are generated by the use of standardized components and elements through the manufacturing and assembly process. Core elements associated with prefabricated architecture are represented by walls, floors, roof and sub-assemblies contained within the building, whether it consists of panelization or modularization or both. Cost- and time-efficiencies are generated when the maximum number of standardized components are integral to the design philosophy for the building. Multiple and repeat production facilitates improved quality throughout the manufacturing and assembly process. Repetition within the manufacturing process, therefore, not only creates economies of scale but also facilitates continued improvements in relation to architectural design, manufacturing quality and refined assembly skills. This feature generates benefits for single building projects, large building projects and especially housing and school projects, where a repetition of house types, teaching spaces, hotel accommodation or student accommodation, for instance, can be exploited to the full but which do not need to be considered as a box-type solution.

The benefits of standardization notwithstanding, a constant debate continues with regard to the attributes and constraints associated with prefabricated architecture which are closely aligned with factory manufacturing and assembly processes more than that of conventional construction practices, which form a dedicated on-site activities-based enterprise. One of the main attributes in support of prefabrication is the ability for the standardized factory manufactured components to provide greater guarantee in quality, consistency, precision and exactness, and to do this repeatedly. Precision and exactness are key features to be expected from the prefabrication process and are more achievable within the factory environment when compared to the changeable conditions associated with the exposed construction site. Rapid advances and increased dependency on machine technology play their part in delivering prefabricated buildings whether it is a

Prefabricated and modular architecture is beyond the perception of repetitive stacked boxes. (Photo by author)

single or multiple building project: they are all reliant on the architect's understanding and his/her ability in applying architectural design principles to the manufacturing and assembly process and especially at concept design stage.

Not all components are manufactured within the one factory. For example, components such as kitchen units, bathroom fittings and furniture or windows and external cladding materials will be sourced from companies and suppliers specializing in those particular materials, parts and components. Similarly, other manufacturing companies specialize in manufacturing wall panel components employed within prefabricated buildings. These specialist wall panel companies differ in the type of wall panel they provide, with different levels of compliance and non-compliance in terms of performance, precision and accuracy. Component design and its manufacture are crucial aspects in the overall prefabricated architecture design and delivery process and it is they that influence the architect's and client's assessment of expected and desired results, all of which are dependent on the capabilities of the manufacturer.

In the context of a building project, panelization is essentially a kit of manufactured components (flat-pack) consisting of wall panels and floor and roof cassettes delivered to the site and installed under the auspices of a normal building contract. A prefabricated modular building, as opposed to panelized construction, takes perceptions of quality and architectural detailing to the next level where the manufacturer is providing a total turnkey project. For modular turnkey buildings, it is the manufacturer who functions as the main contractor who is charged with delivering the entire project which includes foundations, below-ground services and external works, in readiness for the superstructure. With the site-enabling works complete, the modular units are delivered to the site location as high-precision factory-made entities with all components installed and pre-fitted to a high standard ready for the final assemblage to evolve as the modular building envisaged by the architect and the client.

Economies of Scale

Efficiencies derived from standardized components are enhanced when the maximum number of the same standardized components can be used in larger quantities, whether it is for a single building or numerous separate buildings at different times. Multiple replication of the same component adheres to the economies of scale objective. Achieving maximum economies is the goal so the skill of the architect is therefore to employ standardized components as a prerequisite, although it is recognized there is justification for the architect to seek alternative size components where sufficient are required to make it economically viable. Equally, for some components, like windows or specific external cladding panels for instance, a measure of customization will occur by default as a normal part of the process and is priced accordingly.

However, a project designed to adopt a structural insulated panel system for the walls and roof, for example, will benefit more where the maximum number of standardized component panels that can be produced to the same dimensions will provide the most beneficial result. Consequently, with the standard width of a component structural insulated panel at 1,220mm, this is the same width of the oriented strand board (OSB) sheet. The OSB sheet is a component part of the wall panel component; that is, a component part forming the wall panel component (Ung, 2018). Standardization, therefore, is already at work as the manufactured width size of the component wall panel is dictated by the standard size of the OSB sheet from the outset, which is also 1,220mm in width. Following this concept of standardization through to the next level would suggest the length of the wall in the building should be made up by multiples of 1,220mm-wide panels, being the width of the standardized wall panel. Floor and roof cassettes should follow the same reasoning, although the size of floor and roof cassettes is dictated by the span and lifting requirements for the modular unit, the design of which deserves particular attention in the interest of lifting and cost-efficiencies.

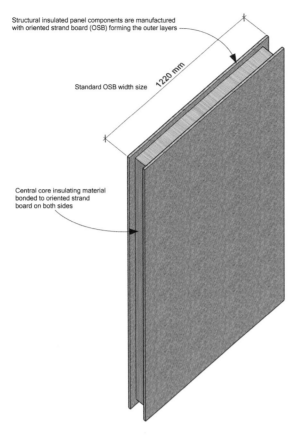

Structural insulated panel components are manufactured with oriented strand board (OSB) forming the outer layers

Standard OSB width size 1220 mm

Central core insulating material bonded to oriented strand board on both sides

Standardized structural insulated panel (SIP). (Courtesy of HOCA Practice)

The length of the wall panel component is dictated by the building's design height, whether it is on-site panelized construction or through the modular build process within the factory. For on-site panelized construction, the length of the component panel can be manufactured to specific sizes to accommodate design height requirements. Panel length requirements are usually dictated by the floor to floor height within the building. This is a flexible situation and facilities within the manufacturing process accommodate variation in panel length to accommodate the height requirements as required by the architect's design. Some structural insulated panel manufacturers offer panel heights of 7m which provide the ability to accommodate two-storey heights in one panel, although 6m is more preferable, usually for performance purposes for certain panel manufacturers.

Other manufacturers will restrict their panel height to 2,440mm which is the length of the standard OSB sheet, thereby capitalizing on the economic benefit generated by the full standardization philosophy. However, current room heights, even for a residential building, now seek floor to ceiling heights in excess of 2,400mm and so an add-on piece is often employed which, in some instances, fails to design out wastage as a prerequisite and attracts useful credits for the project's BREEAM assessment. Modular buildings assembled within a factory environment will have a different set of requirements in relation to standardized lengths. Overall floor heights for the modular unit will usually be in the region of 3,000mm to 3,500mm, depending on where the services are located, and will generally be the same for every module to realize the best economies, which are also reflected by the size of the modular building project.

Standardized System Builds

Current perceptions surrounding prefabricated building generally relate more to the outcome of the factory without any direct engagement of an architect in the design and manufacturing process at any level. Standardized inflexible multi-purpose building solutions such as these are the historic representations associated with the beginning of the last century, where the emphasis lay with satisfying an urgent social need in the most expedient way but with little regard perhaps to aesthetics or architecture as defined today. System build of this nature continues to exist but tends to satisfy a market where the target is focused on buildings for temporary human occupation or buildings where raw functionality and budget pricing is at the forefront in the decision-making process.

For school environments, housing developments and similar community architecture projects where human occupation and context is paramount the situation is somewhat different, although budgetary aspects continue to remain uppermost in decision-makers' thinking. In instances such as these

Prefabricated concrete post and panel building. (Photo by author)

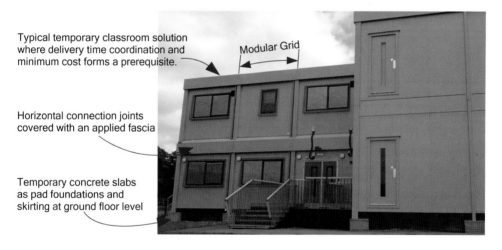

Typical temporary classroom solution where delivery time coordination and minimum cost forms a prerequisite.

Modular Grid

Horizontal connection joints covered with an applied fascia

Temporary concrete slabs as pad foundations and skirting at ground floor level

Standardized modular units set on concrete slabs for foundations. (Photo by author)

the approach of the manufacturer has to be different and indeed it is. Current practice demonstrates a certain level of interaction between the architect and the manufacturer taking place where the manufacturer is selected through a tendering process to provide a design and build turnkey solution. The precise abilities and capabilities of the successful manufacturer and system tendered for tend not to be fully understood and where aspects of quality and architectural detailing are not accounted for in the tender

return it can introduce a measure of discord during the course of the project delivery process, especially when site installation is under way. Situations such as these tend to result, in some cases, in a measure of radical change from the architect's original design in order for the manufacturer to be able to deliver the building: this is especially so in the case of the design and build projects where the potential for a high level of customization by the manufacturer might enter into the mix and override the original design intent.

Modular offices (Medway, UK) based on standardized grid: provision of office accommodation above and storage below is achieved with simple modular container technology. (Photo by author)

Selecting the PAMA Option

There is a growing appetite to substitute PAMA design and manufacturing principles for many of the traditional and conventional forms of building practices so that quality and finishes can be made more predictable and cost-effective and time-efficient alternatives can be provided. Prefabrication, which has existed for over a century, is again being viewed as a means of achieving this objective; where the opportunity exists to see the completed building at the manufacturer's premises this is naturally a big advantage. Examining completed buildings and

customizing preferences before an order is placed establishes a measure of confidence in what is proposed and debunks any element of confusion as to what prefabrication represents or indeed is identified as. For example, the whole range, from standardization and prefabrication to modular panels (panelization), to modular design systems, to modular building and construction, to modular buildings, to off-site manufacture/construction, is all becoming a bit of a muddle for the layperson. Indeed, even among the design fraternity and within its interaction with the construction industry a requirement is generated for better clarification as to what is meant by specific terminology. R.E. Smith (2010) seeks to define a difference between panels for creating interiors (sometimes referred to as modular wall systems) which in

Site-fixing of external cladding system to world's tallest modular apartment building in Croydon, UK. (Photo by author)

New classrooms built over existing roof using modular units with site-fixed external cladding system. (Photo by author)

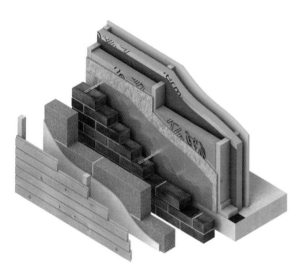

Typical cladding options associated with panelized construction and modular buildings. Brick cladding and block and render finish systems are site-based activities whereas fire-rated metal sheet, timber or other proprietary cladding systems are factory-based processes. (Courtesy of Kingspan Timber Solutions Ltd)

turn should not be confused with modular buildings, which term relates to a completed building.

Notwithstanding the variety of terminologies applied to prefabrication there is a clear distinction between prefabricated architecture and ready-made system build options. Equally too, a clear distinction is drawn between panelization (panelized construction) and modularization (modular buildings) where, in the first instance, component wall, floor and roof panels are recognized more as contributing to the conventional on-site construction process.

Modularization, on the other hand, is represented by volumetric modular units or modules which are premanufactured by assembling parts and components together within a factory environment and dispatched to the site location for completion as a modular assemblage; that is, a modular building. Volumetric modular building, therefore, possesses a very clear and unique characteristic in that it is the only medium to provide up to 95 per cent completion of the building's superstructure from within the factory environment, with the remaining 5 per cent relating to the final assembly process at the site. This, of course, relates to modular buildings where the finished external cladding materials are applied as part of the factory process. In other instances, such as the world's tallest modular apartment building in Croydon in the UK, the external cladding system is applied on-site as an installation process following the assembly of the modular units.

The scope of a building project incorporates aspects surrounding its nature and extent. That is, it embraces the purpose for which it is intended, its size and complexity, its location within the existing built or natural environment, the ease or complexity in relation to mobilizing materials to the site, and any disruption to adjoining properties or other significant features associated with project procurement. The decision to incorporate prefabricated components and the extent of such incorporation are fundamental design decisions for the architect. It dictates whether the building is best delivered through panelization or modularization and thereby is instrumental in determining the building's architecture and ultimately its success aesthetically. Equally significant is the ability for the maximum, if not total, prefabrication to be employed as a means for delivering the architect's design, irrespective of whether panelization or modularization is selected, although panelization possesses greater limitations in terms of delivering a more complete (turnkey) prefabricated building. Nevertheless, the preferred architect design solution should not impede the architect from fully exploiting the opportunities provided by component standardization in delivering his/her final design solution.

Therein rests the skill and ability of the architect to be able to respond to a client's specific instruction and design their functional building as a PAMA solution. In so doing, the architect automatically employs the natural benefits of PAMA while accepting a design discipline dictated more by elements of component standardization relating to manufacturing and assembly processes. But why would an architect choose to design a building through PAMA where a different design discipline prevails, and in many respects an alien one as compared with the familiarities of conventional construction practices? The in-depth nature and extent of such reasoning is a topic in its own right where further exhaustive and highly focused examination is beyond the intention here. For now, though, it is sufficient to highlight where viable alternative cost- and time-efficiencies can be achieved, coupled with contributing significantly to sustainability objectives, to present reason enough for clients to realize their building projects through PAMA.

Equally prevalent is the rejuvenated interest in PAMA ideals, which is already more active perhaps in Europe and in North America than in the UK at present and which is due primarily to the emergence of automation. Once again machine technologies are primed to instigate a new manufacturing revolution perhaps for prefabrication, and hopefully, for this century, architects will become more alert to engaging in an architecture which has the capacity

for advancing 'modern society' in a meaningful way (Anderson and Anderson, 2007). An urgency for PAMA attributes and benefits to be realized with real commitment clearly exists and, at the same time, architects must demonstrate they are truly getting to grips with designing an architecture where manufacturing processes and technologies are totally connected to one another.

Selecting PAMA and Timely Decisions

The essence of whether PAMA as a building procurement route is appropriate for the project is usually a topic with two distinct strands. In the first instance it may be a case where the architect who is an experienced and competent practitioner in prefabricated architecture instinctively knows s/he can deliver the client's building through the PAMA route. Alternatively, it may be the case, given the precise nature, complexity and intended function of the building, where PAMA appropriateness is explored and examined more fully as a natural part of the design concept development.

Within the sphere of delivering a building project through PAMA the numerous processes involved are not monopolized by the architect leading on design issues. The scope and complexity of a building project necessitates the engagement of numerous professionals. The scale and complexity of the building project will naturally dictate the level of design and on-site integration, coordination and timing of project events between the design teams and the on-site operations of the main contractor's team or, where no main contractor participates, the manufacturer, if it is s/he who is charged by the client with the entire on-site delivery process. Fundamental to a successful building project is the ability to make the early decision to either follow a conventional build route or a PAMA build route. The need to deliver timely decisions should be uppermost and such decisions ultimately derive from the architect's concept design process, as alluded to by Taylor et al. (2009). The best situation is always for the client to be equipped with sufficient accurate information from the professional team to act upon, whereby the client is then in a position to make a clear decision for the professional team to follow a totally conventional or a PAMA procurement route.

Failure by the client to provide these timely decisions is the most significant feature for the design, professional and manufacturing teams and their ability to deliver the client's expectations is measured accordingly. Potential disaster awaits when a project is subjected to unnecessary delay. Worst still is a late change in the procurement route in whole or in part following the findings of the project cost analysis which is usually based on the already completed overall design development (detail design) or even tender document information in some instances. (*See also* Chapter 7 under the heading 'Timely Design Decisions'.) Abortive work and potential non-payment also await professional design teams when there are late decisions and abandoned projects.

Integration and Coordination

Integration remains a vital ingredient in any construction project and none more so than when the building project is dominated by the concept of PAMA. It requires the attention of all involved in the project and necessitates the commitment of unity amongst all design, client and manufacturing teams, with a particular emphasis on the main contractor engaging in the construction planning process early in the design stage. Prefabricated design solutions not only need to be appropriate for their context: R.E. Smith (2010, p. 89) affirms also the need for the contractor to have a sound understanding on intent so that s/he may sensibly contribute 'information to the design team regarding general concepts of construction early on', which would suggest the manufacturer would be better placed to function as the main contractor. Very few conventional main contractors are committed to the concept of delivering building projects through PAMA, especially volumetric modular, either through lack of specialized knowledge associated with the process, or because they possess sufficient knowledge to recognize much of their profit potential is consumed by the off-site manufacturer involvement, given that the latter's remit embraces the whole of the superstructure. This is not the situation with panelization, however, where the integrity and ethos of conventional construction practices are maintained.

Enabling works carried out by the main contractor in readiness for lifting and fixing modular units into position by manufacturer. (Courtesy of Structural Timber Projects Ltd)

Modular units 11m long craned into position for final assembly by manufacturer. (Courtesy of Structural Timber Projects Ltd)

Current trends highlight a rare new breed of contractor who already recognizes the advances in PAMA design and technology and its direction for the future, particularly in relation to volumetric modular. They are prepared to embrace the new PAMA science of building where their business focus is directed solely at providing all of the on-site facilities and attendances, including craneage and lifting facilities for the manufacturer's final assembly process. This is true collaboration and cooperation between contractor and manufacturer. Their specific purpose is to undertake all foundation and below-ground services (enabling works) together with all external works and landscaping and to make ready for the manufacturer's final assembly of modular units at the site location. In some instances, depending on the storey height of the building, this specialist contractor will construct the central core areas accommodating the lifts, stairs and service ducts. In essence, they can function either as a main contractor to the client or as a sub-contractor to the client's off-site manufacturer when the manufacturer is appointed as the main contractor. Specialist on-site contractors such as these are instrumental in providing clients with the confidence to make informed decisions relating to committing to PAMA and thus enable manufacturers to focus on all aspects associated with their manufacturing and assembly specialist process. For the architect, too, this approach in delivering PAMA buildings de-risks the overall project management and delivery process and provides an ideal environment for the architect, manufacturer and on-site contractor to collaborate at the front end of the project where client decisions constitute a vital ingredient to the total enterprise.

Chapter Five

Prefabrication Through Panelized Construction

Introduction

Over recent decades in particular, the construction industry has collaborated with off-site manufacturers specializing in wall, floor and roof panel production to promote the use of panelized components in the on-site construction process. For contractors, especially, who are seeking to generate greater efficiencies on-site, particular emphasis lies in options where usual elements and materials are conveniently substituted by prefabricated wall panels as a viable alternative. Whilst substituting elements of the conventional construction process primarily applies to external wall construction it also applies to internal walls. There are numerous manufacturers, not just in the UK, producing wall panels and systems for the various sectors and each advocates their own particular products relative to a specific building use.

From the options available it is not automatically obvious which wall panel systems will provide the best solution for a particular building project, and whether the same should include floor and roof cassettes. It is important for the architect or person designated to select from the various systems available to possess a good understanding as to their compliance with statutory requirements in addition to adhering to cost and life expectations and architectural design suitability. Equally significant is the ability for the decision-maker to possess an intellectual hold at best, or at least a sound appreciation, of the key

Prefabricated architecture delivering bespoke design in the education sector. (Photo by author)

Installing closed panels on a brick plinth for a primary school project. (Photo by author)

considerations surrounding optimal panel dimensions and sizes in relation to the concept design development while remaining mindful as to the attributes associated with standardization.

A primary attribute assigned to current wall panel production is the ability to achieve superior U-values, an inherent feature often promoted for panelization as being more conveniently and economically achieved when compared to conventional construction. Panelization, therefore, tends to have a greater focus on timber and insulation-based materials as opposed to steel or concrete, especially in relation to self-build, community-size building projects and particularly in relation to housing accommodation. Consequently, in the housing market, in particular, on-site timber stick-build was once deemed superior to conventional masonry build as being the viable option to conventional construction but it is now somewhat superseded in many countries by the use of factory-produced panelization where open and closed panels systems, together with structural insulated panel options, are viewed with greater favour.

General Characteristics

In order to appreciate what panelization and panelized construction represent and how they differ from premanufactured modular buildings, it is worth understanding some of the fundamental features and characteristics surrounding the subject. Panelization and panelized construction are defined in a number of ways, are often interpreted differently (sometimes as modular) and consist of numerous options in their composition depending on the intended application/s.

Panelization and Components

The origin of any panelized system is in the materials and parts that make up the components that are manufactured in the first instance. Components are further processed in a predefined method to be transformed into an open or closed panel system or a structural insulated panel system, for example. Each panel system will undergo a particular assembly process specific to it alone. When specific panels are installed together on-site as a standardized system, they are instrumental in forming a space entity, upon which the architect's building design is based in the first place.

The skill of the architect is to arrive at a design where the concept of standardization is employed to the maximum extent with the least number of different component sizes and shapes. Firstly, s/he will have to measure this cost-effective requirement against the architectural result. The second consideration is the fixed modular grid upon which the panel components are arranged (*see* Chapter 4 under the heading 'Structural Grid and PAMA') and set out to the building's design and which is founded on the component's standardized dimensional discipline. The extent to which panelization is used in this way

does not necessarily define the building as a modular building per se but as a panelized building, given the construction process is a dedicated on-site activity as opposed to volumetric modular where totally a manufacturing and assembly process applies. In order for the panel component to contribute to modularity it can only be as a panelized entity. Any subsequent layout arrangement derived from the modularity of the panel component has to be based on its predefined unit of measurement, its geometrical order and discipline to set dimensions as efficiencies in panelization design can be lost if the building consists of non-standard components. The responsibility to maintain a simple and well-defined panelized system rests with the design and manufacturing team from the beginning (R.E. Smith, 2010) so as to negate irregular and complicated component types, and

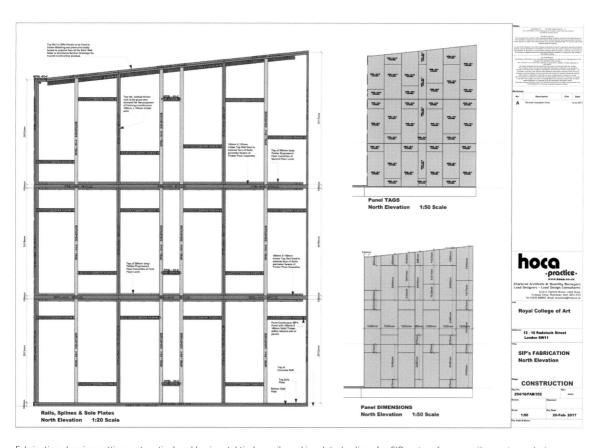

Fabrication drawing setting out vertical and horizontal timber rails and insulated splines for SIP system for a new three-storey design studio in a university building, London. (Courtesy of HOCA Practice)

in this the architect must engage at the front end of the process.

Irrespective of any association panelization may have with or lend to the aesthetic externally, the building may incorporate wall panel components primarily to expedite the conventional build process in seeking to achieve improved efficiencies and practicalities of construction. For example, a conventional brick and block cavity wall construction may be substituted in part by a panelized wall alternative for the inner leaf.

Panelization is also used in conjunction with a steel-framed structure where the wall panels form

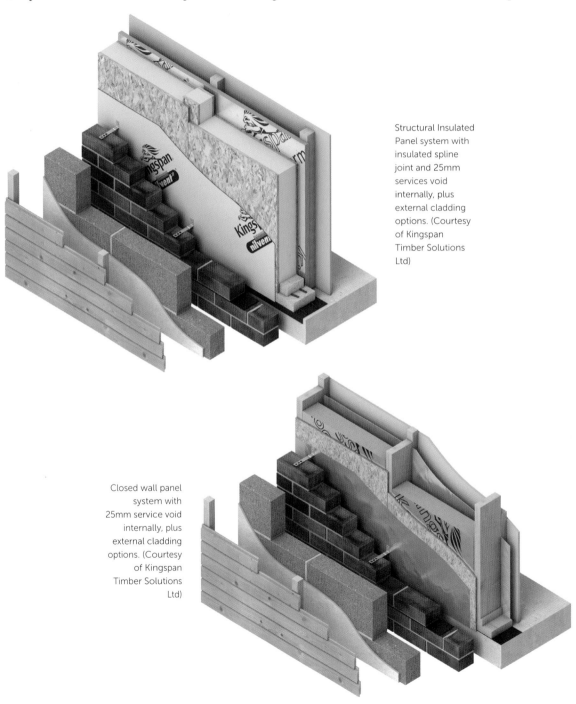

Structural Insulated Panel system with insulated spline joint and 25mm services void internally, plus external cladding options. (Courtesy of Kingspan Timber Solutions Ltd)

Closed wall panel system with 25mm service void internally, plus external cladding options. (Courtesy of Kingspan Timber Solutions Ltd)

Steel frame building with SIP system as external wall for timber battening and external rainscreen cladding system. (Photo by author)

the main wall construction; the outer cladding (such as a brick outer leaf) is then tied into this or the outer cladding system is fixed directly to it (such as a proprietary rainscreen cladding system).

As an entity then, the wall panels become a set piece of the building as in the conventional sense. However, although buildings or parts of buildings constructed through panelization are often referred to as 'modular' building this is not really the case. In reality, the word 'modular' is often borrowed by wall panel manufacturers and others because 'modular' as an expression is fashionable. Some consider that, since wall panel components are manufactured within a factory environment, the term therefore bestows some semblance of authenticity to 'modular buildings', but it does not in circumstances such as those highlighted above.

Nevertheless, in reality, this notion of 'modular' relates primarily to the repetition of the wall panels' standardized sizes, such as structural insulated panels for example, and in others a multiplicity of panel sizes which are not modularized nor even standardized, such as closed panels, as these are often bespoke panel sizes for a given location for a given project, often with their own unique specification inclusions. Whilst they are employed in the architecture of the building they are not usually expressed as modular space in the aesthetic of the building. In other words, panelization is used as a building material in a conventional on-site construction process. At most, this panelized element alone could only sensibly be defined as off-site manufacturing (OSM), but the entire building could not reasonably be described as a 'modular building', unlike a modular building produced from a factory-premanufactured three-dimensional modular unit.

The modularity of wall panels themselves, however, is a feature not to be ignored by the architect at the concept design stage as economies are achieved by designing to the modularity of the standard component sizes, where the same is a primary feature of the wall panel system. There is, therefore, a clear distinction between panelized modularity, insofar as it relates to a modular or standardized panel component only, and the modularity associated with a true three-dimensional premanufactured 'volumetric modular building' as in the PAMA sense. Further, with panelization employed as a substitute material, the legitimacy of 'shell and core' promoted as 'modular building' is also not valid as this is deemed to be panelized construction. True 'modular buildings', on the other hand, are defined as three-dimensional volumetric modular entities; that is, where volumetric modular units or modules are premanufactured, assembled and fitted out as a complete entity within a factory environment, dispatched to the site location and assembled there, where the final assemblage forms a complete modular building. Referring to modular building and modular construction as an on-site activity, therefore, ceases to be valid or relay accurate meaning on this basis as panelized construction constitutes building or constructing with panels.

Wall Panel Composition

Internally, and depending on the wall panel system, provision can be made within the wall panel to accommodate electrical services and light switch locations. Some wall panel manufacturers exalt the benefits associated with electrical services inclusion within their closed wall panel system as a means to distinguish their system from those of competitors. Whilst this feature might appear attractive and in keeping with the notion surrounding modern methods of construction the reality is somewhat different. In essence, as a first-fix element, the high level of advanced coordination bestowed on the manufacturer is a risk factor worth removing; instead it should be placed with experienced electrical installers on-site who are under the direct control of the main contractor as part of the conventional process. Furthermore, penetrations into the structural element of a closed wall panel through the fire and acoustic layers can threaten their respective ratings for the closed wall panel originally designed for, as well as having a potential impact on the wall panel's structural performance. Avoiding any penetrations into the structural closed wall panel is the best option and can be achieved by applying timber battens to the face of the closed wall panel, which achieves a number of preferred options. It creates a clear service zone, usually 25mm, for electrical and other services to be accommodated in the first instance. More fundamental, however, is the ability to accommodate the depth required for light switches and sockets which should never penetrate the fire and acoustic outer layers of the closed panel, although sometimes they do.

Panelized Shell and Core

Panelization, though, is often used to provide a complete shell and core solution for the building's superstructure where all of the external and internal wall panels, together with the floor and roof cassettes, form the building's structure, its external envelope and internal space arrangements. Shell and core means, therefore, a building which is not complete; that is, it is essentially an empty shell as it does not have all the building services or finishes or external wall cladding or roof finishes. The 'core' element normally associated with a shell and core approach relates to the central circulation zone within the building such as the lift and stairs area, central toilets, stores, electrical cupboards and the like: this would apply to school or office buildings, for example. In residential buildings similar core areas would apply to apartment buildings whereas in a single house the core would consist of the main stairs areas.

Shell and core through panelization provide an ideal opportunity for the architect to design buildings which are of a bespoke nature where room spaces are unique if required. In this instance, there is a valid case to classify this form of building as a 'fabricated' building through panelization as the only elements that are prefabricated in a factory are the actual panels. The actual construction, the final fit-out and finishes are completed by the main contractor on-site in the conventional way. In more recent times, some manufacturers have elected to undertake the completion and fit-out of the building on-site also as part of their overall package with the client, thereby negating the need for a conventional main contractor and making the manufacturer's overall design and build package attractive.

In many panelized buildings the wall panels function as the structural walls and are capable of carrying upper floors. Depending on the size of the panelized building, its complexity and structural performance requirements, certain wall panel systems may not be capable of providing sufficient structural support for

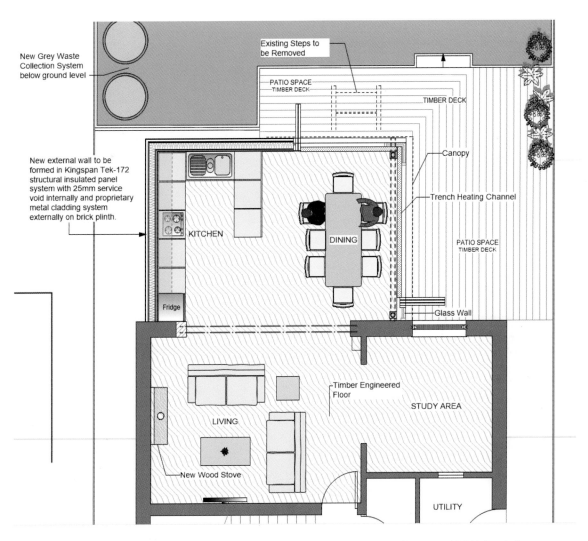

Typical plan using standardized SIPs 1,220mm wide for a new single-storey residential addition. (Courtesy of HOCA Practice)

the anticipated use of the building with its intended loads. In such cases, laminated timber beams or steel beams and posts are introduced to perform that function, but then the validity and appropriateness of that particular prefabricated wall panel system under consideration for the building has to be questioned. Moreover, the rationale surrounding a totally panelized building which is so oversubscribed with independent beam and column support to justify the design solution also has to be questioned. Perhaps it is cost- and/or time-saving efficiencies promoted by the manufacturer that make the option attractive and validate continuance. Or perhaps it is sheer vanity on somebody's part. Whatever reasoning behind such a decision it is, notwithstanding, fraught with risk associated with design coordination, construction difficulties and unknowns, which if properly scrutinized from the outset will probably highlight good reason not to pursue that particular option.

Wall Panel Manufacture

The essence of panelization is represented by wall panels which are manufactured and assembled in a factory, either as a standardized system specific and unique to a particular manufacturer or perhaps where a number of manufacturers make a similar panel product but with different materials providing different performance and durability features. Wall panel manufacturers produce a standardized external and internal wall panel product which is designed to target a number of typical applications. They also seek to demonstrate how their bespoke panel design might accommodate numerous applications to a degree,

Extensive use of steel columns and beams questions the validity of using closed wall panels systems as an appropriate architectural design solution. (Photo by author)

albeit with a level of adjustment to the panel composition and its dimensions. Generally, manufacturers provide external and internal wall panel options where a ready-made market already exists, primarily based on the manufacturers' existing factory processes which are already tried and tested and geared up for what is potentially the mainstay of their business activities.

Manufacturers tend not to engage in producing bespoke, newly invented, one-off wall panel solutions only; that is, wall panels of a highly bespoke and specialist nature. Bespoke panel production of this kind would first go through a process of prototype manufacture in conjunction with rigorous testing to ensure suitability, appropriateness and, more importantly, accreditation (*see* Chapter 7) for such an enterprise to demonstrate value. In truth, it is rare and indeed financially not viable for the architect to invent new panel components for their specific building projects. Having a focus on options which already exist is usually a more viable option. Where further specification enhancement is required, to achieve specific fire and acoustic ratings or specific finishes for aesthetic reasons perhaps, adjustments can be made to the composition of the panel and material selection. The architect, therefore, should not expect a manufacturer to produce a totally unique wall panel entity for his/her single building except, perhaps, where extremely large quantities are involved, as with projects such as large housing developments, for instance, where standardized panels and multiple repetition would form a significant feature in generating sufficient cost-efficiencies.

Standard Panel Manufacture

Currently, the uniqueness of each manufacturer's panelized system will normally apply to a number of possible project types. Their product is inclined to remain unchanged, having created a view of the market and identified where their particular wall panel is placed within it. For example, a closed panel system can work equally as well for a house project as a school, as indeed will a structural insulated panels system solution. Variations in height, length and thickness can be entertained by the manufacturer (customization) to accommodate the building's design, albeit with a measure of limitation for some panel systems dictated primarily by panels' performance requirements in the case of some wall panels or transportation reasons for others, perhaps. It is the simplicity and ease with which the wall panel system can be applied to the overall project and not just the actual building in isolation that will determine the real effectiveness of the system under consideration, if budget and time are primary factors. It is incumbent upon the architect to identify which of the existing wall panel systems available best suits his/her objectives, and, at the same time, seek perhaps to improve the wall panel's performance and durability by its use in a particular way or by adding value to the panel's design and component composition in a unique manner without undermining cost-efficiencies already well established by the manufacturer. There are, of course, benefits, attributes and constraints associated with each wall panel system. The appropriate panel required for a building project therefore is informed by the general features of the building design, specific design detailing, performance requirements, delivery dates and, indeed, personal preferences.

Maximum efficiencies and cost benefits are best achieved for a given project where the manufacturer can produce the wall panels to a standard size and with multiple repetition where possible. Where closed or open panels are deemed to be the most appropriate choice for the building the architect should seek to design his/her building with an optimum size panel for standardization and create the required room spaces accordingly. Structural insulated panel (SIP) building systems, on the other hand, are products where the panels are already manufactured to a standard width size (*see* Chapter 4), thereby establishing a design discipline for the architect in relation to the wall length created by multiples of the standard panel width. Varying lengths and heights are a recipe for potential mishaps, both in the manufacturing process and with on-site construction, where tolerance levels for fabricated and modular components should be superior to that of conventional construction. Architectural design which embraces a standard regime does not impede the creation of flexible spatial arrangements for the building, irrespective of whether the wall panel consists of open and closed panel or SIP construction system. Standard panels and sizes with as much repetition as possible do introduce a design discipline synonymous with the PAMA philosophy.

Technical Know-How and Specification

Some wall panel manufacturers view the production of wall panels as relocating a part of the on-site construction activity to within the factory but in actuality a distinct difference exists between panelized construction and construction using hand trades. The objective for panelization is to bring the benefits of high-quality finished components from the factory environment to the site where exactness and precision are deemed to be a prerequisite. Delivering panels to the site from a factory with tolerances of anything up to 20mm is futile and offers no improvement or benefit to the contractor on-site as these tolerance levels already exist using hand trade methods. Rectifying and adjusting the building's geometry by having to correct and adjust inaccurate panel components is a contractor's nightmare as it is an opportunity for additional costs to creep in. Making allowances to accommodate finished joinery, door and window installation and final fit-out of the building will be a prevalent feature and a constant battle for the contractor seeking to deliver a good-quality finished building, which is not what panelized construction is meant to represent. Manufacturers who fail to deliver their panelized components with tolerances of not more than 2mm fail to contribute to the concept of prefabricated and modular architecture. Without this level of expectation in panel component production the concept of prefabricated building through panelization becomes less attractive, if indeed viable.

Defective panel production does little to enhance the perception of quality, precision and exactness. (Photo by author)

Panelization is applied to buildings in many sectors, each with its own particular performance and specification requirements, and it is for the architect to know and understand which of the systems available will best suit his/her particular building for their client. Very often, the attributes of a particular system are promoted by the manufacturers themselves, omitting perhaps to highlight what constraints or limitations might exist for a given situation. Equally significant will be the degree to which particular panel systems are completed within the factory and to what extent. Confusion for the specifier/decision-maker often transpires when seeking to identify the option that is best value for money with regard to pre-finished panels. For example, the architect should appreciate if the project will be more economic where a particular manufacturer provides a closed panel system with all insulation and electrical services installed, complete with putty pad fire protection where appropriate, as a more complete system than an open panel system where insulation and electrical installations are completed by the contractor on-site. Equally, s/he should have a good comprehension as to what level of performance is required and the capacity for the selected panel system to provide the same. Whether the project will be delivered more quickly and economically where much of the work is completed within the factory compared to that completed by the contractor on-site requires further consideration, a factor which is usually of prime importance to the client. Understanding what the right questions are to ask for a given building project is vital therefore and being able to analyse which option presents the best value for money is key for most clients. In this regard there is a process for the architect to follow. It is important, therefore, for adequate time to be

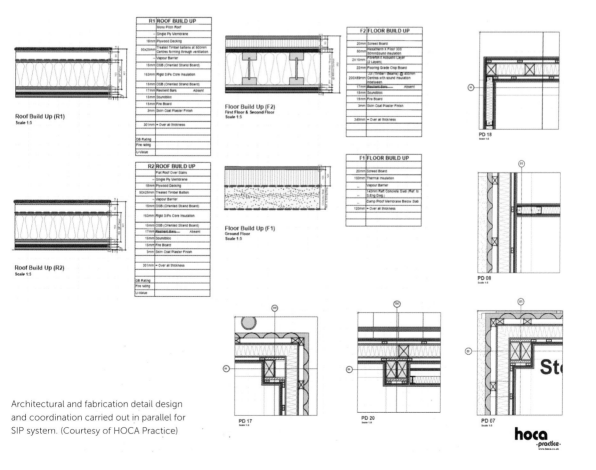

Architectural and fabrication detail design and coordination carried out in parallel for SIP system. (Courtesy of HOCA Practice)

allowed in the project timetable to assess the market and complete a proper analysis from the beginning and as part of the concept design development for the building project.

Open and Closed Wall Panels

Modern high-tech manufacturing and assembly machinery continues to evolve in catering for the ever-increasing demands placed on PAMA building in the UK and the higher requirements placed on manufacturing precision and exactness are expected to be met in equal measure. Manufacturers need to be more alert to the high demands and expectations of clients and architects where the industry is already mobilizing to move away from the factory hand-built approach to full automation. Wild variations in dimensions and inaccurate panel manufacture are

aspects normally associated with the on-site environment but are no longer appropriate or indeed tolerated for the new science surrounding PAMA projects.

Open Wall Panel Construction

Open panel construction consists of timber studding forming the primary structure which is nail-fixed to rigid sheathing usually made of standard size (imperial 8ft × 4ft or metric 2,440mm × 1,220mm) plywood or OSB sheets. The rigid sheathing prevents 'racking', which is the term used to describe a panel tilting when its structural components are forced out of plumb, commonly caused by wind applying horizontal pressure. To prevent racking, plywood or OSB sheathing of an appropriate grade and thickness provides the necessary bracing to the panel which might otherwise have to be provided by diagonal bracing, a

Precision and exactness with machine automation. (Courtesy of Frame Homes (SW) Ltd)

traditional method referred to as 'let-in' or 'diagonal strap' bracing. The timber studs and rigid sheathing, when correctly assembled, function together to form the structural integrity of the panel and it is crucial for the status of the panel to remain damage-free from the point of manufacture to the completion of the installation on-site.

The word 'open' means exactly that. It is open on one side: only one side of the timber studding is clad with rigid sheathing and nothing else. The open panel arrives on the site from the factory and is installed into the works like any other material element. Panelized construction projects using open panels form part of the on-site construction process and are now more commonly associated with one-off and small domestic-scale projects. Structural performance requirements are dictated by loadings which will determine the size of the timber studding. In most instances the open panel is used as a structural element substituting for the more traditional materials used (as in traditional cavity wall construction). Initially, open panel construction was used to substitute for the inner masonry leaf of a traditional cavity wall but more recently the whole of the open panel is designed for structural performance primarily, thereby negating the need to use conventional masonry construction. The thermal, fire and acoustic performances and so on are only achieved with the completion of the insulation and internal plasterboard layers on-site by the contractor.

Within the UK open timber panel systems have had a notable presence in the housing market since the early 1970s. Their ability to offer enhanced performance in terms of improved efficiency in heat loss control and cost savings became apparent and in many cases they were adopted as worthy alternatives to conventional masonry building practice. U-value requirements for walls, floors and roofs have been constantly changing to meet rising performance standards, thereby necessitating an increased thickness of insulation. Consequently, the timber studding now employed for the open panel has changed from the previous 38mm × 90mm timber studs to a minimum 38mm × 140mm deep, where the space

between the studding is filled to the full depth of 140mm with insulation as an on-site activity carried out by the contractor.

Within the context of prefabrication and open panel construction in particular, it is difficult to defend the case for using open panels as the minimum amount of factory-based manufacturing is involved. Compared to other panel construction options which embrace both thermal and/or acoustic requirements as part of the manufacturing process, open panel construction does little to contribute to the PAMA ethos in a meaningful way. There is already a growing demand to create greater efficiencies and removing as much construction activity away from the site to the manufacturing environment is considered the correct approach. Open panel construction struggles to deliver persuasive reasons to justify its place as a method of construction. (*See* 'Panelization and Extent of Use' below.)

Greater demands are now being placed on design requirements for new buildings. As such, panelization must demonstrate its capacity for managing the very essence of architectural design detail where the primary considerations are:

- structural performance
- control of water penetration
- airtightness, thermal performance
- acoustics performance
- vapour control.

Basic ingredients such as these must be catered for in the PAMA design philosophy with equal efficiency, if not better, when compared to conventional design and construction practice. These features, however, do not form an obvious part of the open panel manufacturing process and consequently, for a building to be compliant to current building regulations and codes, significant work remains for the contractor to complete on-site which, for the contractor, generates greater profit potential and is perhaps the reason why open panel construction is popular with the smaller contractor or the self-builder. The extent to which open panel construction offers itself as an obvious choice within the sphere of PAMA design is somewhat limited, if indeed valid, given that its core function and physical features are more representative of the conventional construction process.

Closed Wall Panel Construction

The closed wall panel is the opposite to the open wall panel in that its design and manufacture are somewhat different. Whilst the open and closed wall panel are often classified together as timber-frame or off-site construction in a global sense, there are distinct differences between the two, displayed by their composition and intended purpose. Both types of wall panel use timber studs with OSB sheathing generally to perform structurally, albeit to varying degrees, but there ends any sensible comparison between the two as their respective compositions and performance capabilities differ radically. Unlike the open wall panel concept the closed wall panel is designed to take manufacturing to another dimension and, at the same time, expedite the work by minimizing the construction time on the site even more. In essence, closed wall panels are extolled not only as a means for removing even more of the on-site activities associated with conventional construction, but when compared to the open wall panel they also

demonstrate the evolution of more intensified factory manufacturing and assembly processes in relation to panelized construction and PAMA generally.

The principal feature of the closed panel is represented by material elements which go into the manufacture and assembly of the entire panel component within the factory environment. The innovativeness and vision of the manufacturer in graduating from open panel to closed panel is often symbolized by the degree to which his/her factory is mechanized and automated to accommodate predicted growth in prefabrication within construction. Indeed, the description 'closed', as tagged to the panel name, is derived from the manufacturing process where the timber studs form the central core of the panel with sheathing material applied to both sides of the timber studs, thereby effectively closing off the timber studs, the vapour control layer/barrier, the insulation and (in some cases) the electrical services within. Whilst OSB sheathing is the usual material applied to the external side of the panel, primarily for cost-efficiencies, the internal side is usually finished with combinations of plasterboard so as to provide a final finish for decorating purposes. The plasterboard sheathing is either for fire or acoustic rating purposes or both and is specified by the architect who is experienced in selecting the correct fire resistance or decibel (db)

Factory-manufactured closed wall panel with pre-fitted window and protective breather membrane being installed on top of the brick plinth. (Photo by author)

Complete wall panel sections with factory fitted windows lifted into position for fixing to top of brick plinth and left ready for external cladding system

Breather membrane folded over and staple fixed to adjoining panel to form seal

Metal strap fixing to anchor closed wall panel to top of brick plinth rating deemed appropriate for a particular space or function within a space.

Specifying the materials for a closed wall panel is more involved than that for an open wall panel. It is more complex as it must comply with standards and requirements associated with specific building types and functions. Equally significant is the manner in which the wall panel component as an entity fits into the fabric of the building and is designed to take its place within the building's architecture in a very precise, exact and prescribed way. The architect is trained to be demanding and to possess a sharper focus in relation to what is good architectural detailing for satisfying building regulations, codes, standards and, essentially, good building practice. Equally important for the architect is to ensure the building's geometry presents the correct aesthetic for its given context; where the manufactured wall panels are employed as a vehicle for architectural expression to that end, prefabrication is judged accordingly.

The architect, therefore, is expected to have a well-rounded approach to the final design and delivery of the building where these characteristics are evidenced through panelization. It is demonstrated most forcefully where the detail of architectural design is co-joined with all aspects of the fabrication design in parallel and under the one design leadership, thereby negating potential design clash and coordination issues. For instance, closed wall panels have the ability to accommodate the installation of the external doors and windows as part of the total factory process. Under the auspices of PAMA, panelization and DfMA are natural companions in practice as their interfaces form the crux of correct detail design where function and aesthetic are under scrutiny. Interfaces such as doors and window frames with that of the internal and external finishes, for instance, are typical connection points and are best designed in parallel as a natural all-inclusive design process embracing airtightness and cold bridging. Further examples would be the interface of the closed wall panel with the external cladding or the form of the roof with that of the external wall. There are many facets of the building's detail design where architectural and fabrication design must coexist in a sympathetic and harmonious manner, both functionally and aesthetically. The skill to be able to design for both specialisms and disciplines in unison must therefore rest with the architect, where PAMA architectural and fabrication design reign jointly as the bedrock of design for manufacturing and assembly (DfMA).

Considering panelization as the appropriate solution for the building is one milestone in the design analysis; deciding on which type of panelization is the

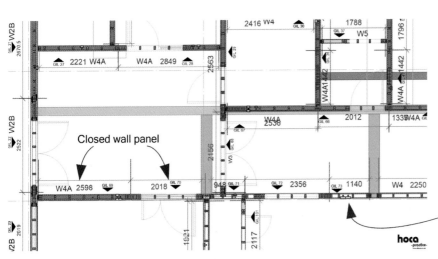

Closed wall panels functioning as internal structural walls, compartment walls and partition walls

Closed wall panels accommodating recessed electrical power sockets, switch sockets and conduits must ensure the integrity of the fire rating for the wall panel is maintained using 'putty pad' protection or similar.

Plan arrangement using closed wall panels. (Courtesy of HOCA Practice)

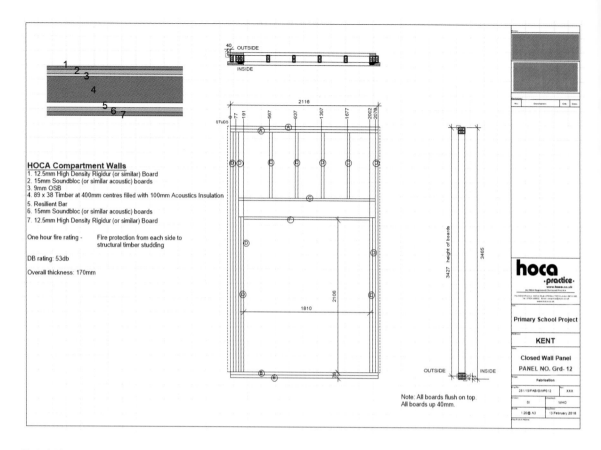

Typical fabrication drawing for closed wall panel. (Courtesy of HOCA Practice)

Robust detailing for closed wall panel construction. (Courtesy of HOCA Practice)

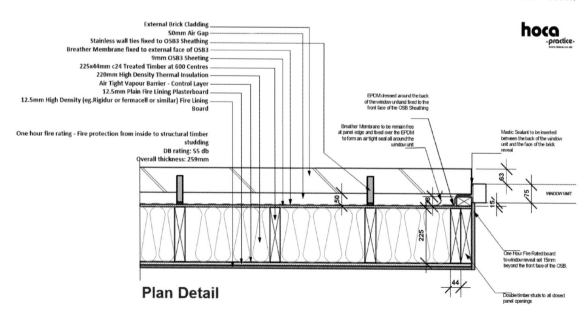

next matter to resolve. Whilst there are numerous distinct features and characteristics which relate to both open and closed wall panel construction there are some common considerations that apply to them both. One instance might be the length of the wall panel for a given location within the fabric of the building and how it is best placed on the delivery vehicle to utilize space to the maximum. Another might be whether the panels should be placed flat or in a vertical position for transporting from the factory to the site.

Protective Wrap

The external face of the OSB sheathing that is fixed to the timber studs needs to be protected from the elements as soon as possible, preferably as part of the manufacturing process and especially where OSB is used in the manufacture of the panel. Protection is provided by applying a breather membrane, sometimes referred to as a breathable membrane or a protective wrap. Whilst the breather membrane is usually applied to the external face of the panel as part of the factory manufacturing process there are some occasions when it is more convenient to apply it on-site. The breather membrane has two functions: firstly, it provides a protective layer to the OSB sheathing in

particular and the fabric of the open panel in general should any point of the external cladding fail; secondly, it acts as a second line of defence and protection to the panel where its structural integrity is of paramount importance.

Similar issues such as accuracy and quality control and how the most efficient use of structural timber for the studding is managed are all topics which relate to both open and closed panel construction. The primary consideration for the architect specifying products and building systems, however, is to evaluate the attributes and constraints associated with alternative options and in this regard the structural insulated panel provides an obvious choice.

Mid Floors and Cassettes

Panelization also embraces the manufacture of floors and roofs too, referred to as floor and roof cassettes in the case of timber-based components, which, together with wall panels, allow complete buildings to be designed, manufactured and delivered to the site as 'flat-pack', thus providing a shell and core for installation. Essentially, it is a kit of parts and a means for creating the structure of the building on-site more rapidly compared to conventional build practice. Panelization, whilst sometimes incorrectly referred

Premanufactured floor cassette being lifted into position for a new building using SIPs. (Courtesy of Kingspan TEK Building System)

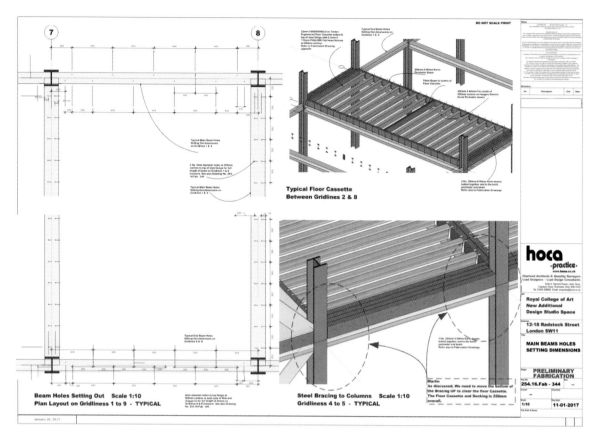

Fabrication and architectural design in parallel demonstrate robust design coordination throughout. (Courtesy of HOCA Practice)

to as modular under the generic term, does not offer a complete turnkey solution for the client as is the case with volumetric modular as discussed in Chapter 6.

Structural Insulated Panel (SIP) Building Systems

Differentiating SIP from SIPS

The identity of the structural insulated panel (SIP) lies in its distinctiveness as an insulated composite panel when compared to the open or closed panel system in particular. Both building systems evolved from different factory manufacturing processes. Whilst both building systems are recognized within the construction industry generally, the degree to which the specific features of each system respond to specific requirements is less obvious. Both begin their existence by establishing a place in the superstructure of a building as a prefabricated panelized component and whereas the closed panel has a predetermined purpose by the manner in which it is used, the SIP can function in two distinct ways. Firstly, the structural insulated panel building system (SIPS) functions as a self-supporting structural building system capable of creating the superstructure for buildings up to four storeys high. Secondly, the SIP can take panelization to a further level when employed as cladding to a separate structural frame of a building to provide the external perimeter walls. There are a number of SIP manufacturers and not all work to the same accredited standard with BBA certified approval (see Chapter 7, 'Certified Approvals'). The

Structural insulated panel with recessed edge ready for timber rails or insulated splines. (Courtesy of Kingspan Timber Solutions Ltd, photo by author)

Complete wall panel sections factory-assembled using an SIP building system and now being installed at the site. (Courtesy of Kingspan Timber Solutions Ltd)

manner in which SIP as a panel and SIPS as a building system perform within the fabric of a building is determined by their respective properties and how they measure up to offering the architect choices in terms of functionality, cost- and time-efficiencies, freedom of design, architectural detailing, robustness, thermal and acoustic performance, airtightness, speed of installation and similar characteristics.

SIP and SIPS with a Difference

There are different types of SIP products produced by various manufacturers, each with different characteristics and performance levels. For instance, SIP products can vary in overall thickness where the insulated central core is dictated by the overall thickness of the OSB skins forming the outer skins of the panel. The thermal performance of the panel, too, will be influenced by the insulation material used and its thickness, which can be as little as 78mm and up to 288mm as standard panel sizes. A standard produced panel is always the better option when seeking to control the project budgets. Certain manufacturers tend to produce a number of panel thicknesses as their standard sizes in order to fulfil project criteria that they would envisage. Other manufacturers, however, provide less thickness choice in their standard panel range primarily because they are satisfied their SIP product, which is an element of their particular building system, is certified by the BBA or similar approval body and, as such perhaps, will perform in a superior manner and be satisfactory to the architect's design requirements. The make-up and performance of panel components, both structural and thermal, can differ between manufacturers, as

Kingspan Insulation Ltd

Pembridge
Leominster
Herefordshire HR6 9LA

Tel: 01544 387382 Fax: 01544 387482

e-mail: technical@kingspantek.co.uk

website: www.kingspantek.co.uk

Agrément Certificate
02/S029
Product Sheet 1

KINGSPAN STRUCTURAL INSULATED PANEL (SIP) SYSTEMS

KINGSPAN TEK BUILDING SYSTEM

This Agrément Certificate Product Sheet[1] relates to the Kingspan TEK Building System, loadbearing wall and roof panels comprising Structural Insulated Panels (SIPs) manufactured from OSB/3 and rigid urethane insulation. The system is for use above the damp-proof course in domestic applications up to four storeys high as the loadbearing inner leaf of an external cavity wall or as part of separating walls, internal loadbearing walls, and flat and pitched roofs.

(1) Hereinafter referred to as 'Certificate'.

CERTIFICATION INCLUDES:

- factors relating to compliance with Building Regulations where applicable
- factors relating to additional non-regulatory information where applicable
- independently verified technical specification
- assessment criteria and technical investigations
- design considerations
- installation guidance
- regular surveillance of production
- formal three-yearly review.

Certification and industry approval is available from a number of bodies. The document sets out what the certification includes and identifies the key factors associated with the individual product or building system. (Courtesy of Kingspan TEK Building System)

indeed can their building system, which consists of both panels and other components of various types and descriptions. Some manufacturers only provide the insulated panel and not the complete system; that is, all the other components required to install the superstructure of the building at the site. In these situations, the manner in which the building system is put together is left to the building contractor.

SIP represents the actual panel component, and the manner in which the panel itself will perform as a part of the building system is dictated by the materials used in its manufacturing or assembly process. Crucial aspects associated with SIP manufacture revolve around the

materials used to form the central insulation core, the grade and thickness of the OSB outer skins and, most importantly, the manner in which the OSB skins are bonded to the insulated core. Equally significant for the central insulated core, therefore, is the potential difference in thermal conductivity between polyurethane rigid foam (PUR) and polyisocyanurate (that is, rigid polyiso foam or PIR) and polystyrene (PS). A material's thermal conductivity is the number of Watts conducted per metre thickness of the material, per degree of temperature difference between one side and the other (W/mK). As a rule of thumb, the lower the thermal conductivity the better, because the material conducts less heat energy. A difference in thermal conductivity means therefore, that the insulation core with a lower (better) thermal conductivity will achieve the same U-value across a smaller cross-section (thinner board) than a board with a worse thermal conductivity. Panels made with PUR insulation achieve the same U-value across a smaller cross-section (thinner panel) than a panel employing PS insulation. The physical bond between the OSB skins and the insulated core is a key feature for an SIP, and where a potential for debonding of the two materials exists the structural integrity of the SIP is seriously at risk. Consequently, autohesively bonding the insulation to the OSB skins as a manufacturing process to create a SIP component, as opposed to gluing the rigid insulation to the OSB as an assembly process, is a significant feature of the SIP's characteristic and worthy of note for the architect. The architect should be satisfied as to the reliability of the panel manufacturing process and whether it will stand up to industry-standard testing, certification procedures and validation. Appropriate investigation and research is recommended as to how the bonding of the insulation to the OSB skins is achieved for the SIP, and the extent to which the same is certified by the BBA or similar bodies as part of an approved system.

Designing for Manufacture and Assembly (DfMA)

The nature and extent of the complete building system required for a project is determined by the architect as a natural progression of the architectural design process. Specialist fabrication design drawings prepared by the architect are in a format for the manufacturer to convert to manufacturing production. Computer aided design/computer aided manufacture (CAD/CAM) applications are used to both design the building and programme the manufacturing process in a fully automated factory environment where computer numerical control (CNC) machinery plays a vital role. CNC machinery supersedes machines requiring manual control where hitherto human interaction guided and prompted the commands of machine tools via levers, buttons, wheels, bells and whistles.

Architect's design detail and SIP fabrication design and detailing as one design exercise. (Courtesy of HOCA Practice)

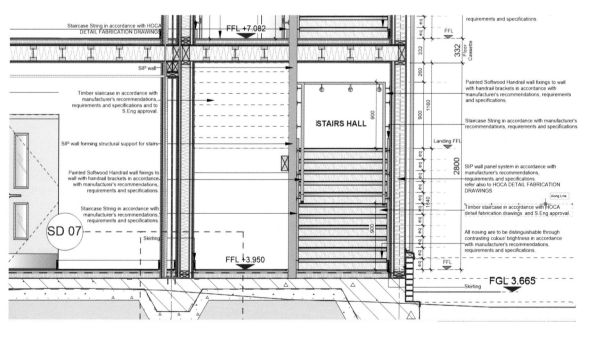

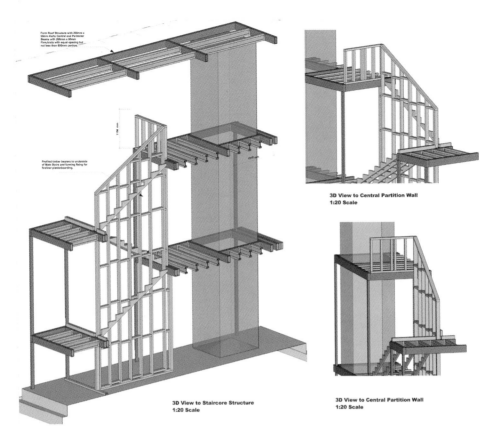

3D View to Central Partition Wall
1:20 Scale

3D View to Staircore Structure
1:20 Scale

3D View to Central Partition Wall
1:20 Scale

3D View to Central Partition Wall
1:20 Scale

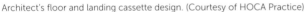

Architect's floor and landing cassette design. (Courtesy of HOCA Practice)

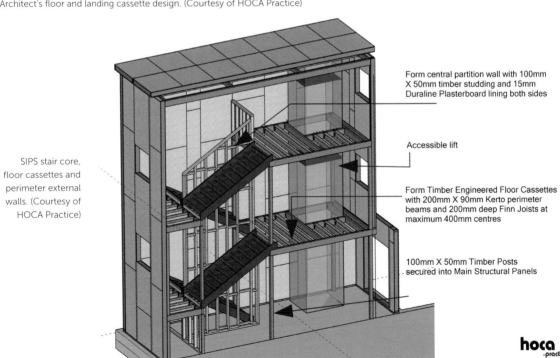

Form central partition wall with 100mm
X 50mm timber studding and 15mm
Duraline Plasterboard lining both sides

Accessible lift

SIPS stair core,
floor cassettes and
perimeter external
walls. (Courtesy of
HOCA Practice)

Form Timber Engineered Floor Cassettes
with 200mm X 90mm Kerto perimeter
beams and 200mm deep Finn Joists at
maximum 400mm centres

100mm X 50mm Timber Posts
secured into Main Structural Panels

hoca
·practice·

Approved Contractors

As with any construction project it is always wise to consider contractors who can demonstrate their ability to understand the design proposed by the architect and to execute the works at the site in a competent and efficient manner. Membership of the UK's Chartered Institute of Builders (CIOB) is a good measure of the capabilities of contractors and builders in this regard. The same applies where specialist contractors are best employed to carry out specialist work. Building in SIPS is a specialist enterprise and requires a level of expertise in appreciating the science which lies behind why and how the various components are designed to be assembled in a particular way.

The SIP, whilst a most significant ingredient within the concept of SIPS construction and technology, is often considered and evaluated in isolation and not in the context of the overall building system. The panel,

albeit a standardized multi-produced component available with numerous OSB and insulated core thicknesses, only represents one entity of SIPS. It is nonetheless dependent upon working in conjunction with other components to be an effective building system. Some manufacturers specialize in just manufacturing the panel and do not engage in providing components to make up a complete building system as their business essentially is to manufacture and sell the panels. It is therefore left to the devices of the contractor operating in an independent capacity to undertake the building project; they may or may not have adequate knowledge and experience in building with SIPS or perhaps may have even less understanding of what SIPS is as a building system.

SIP fabrication drawings extracted from architect's CAD model. (Courtesy of HOCA Practice)

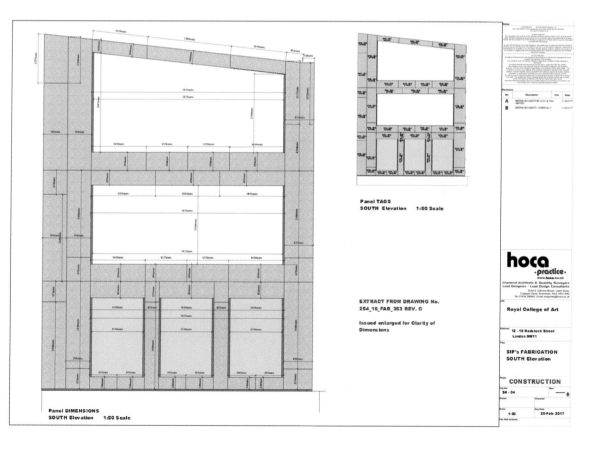

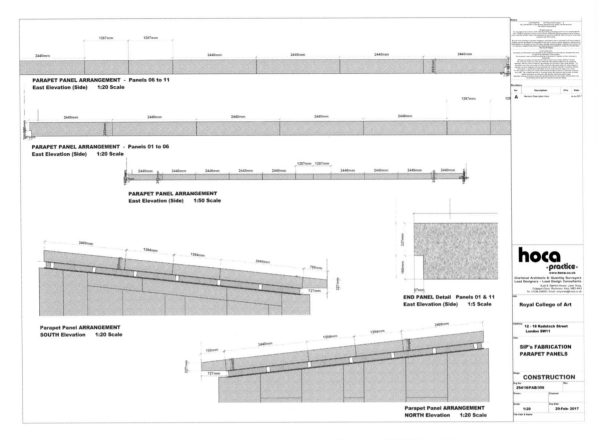

Panel component fabrication drawings prepared for CNC cutting machinery. (Courtesy of HOCA Practice)

Diagram of SIPS
construction
project linking into
existing building.
(Courtesy of HOCA
Practice)

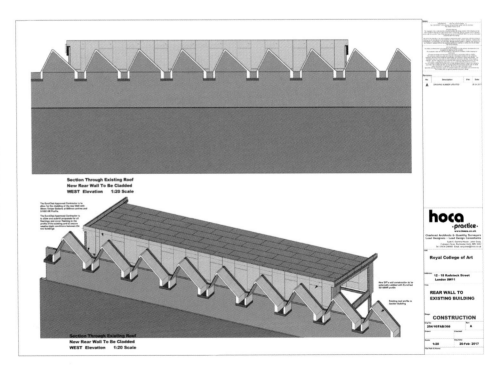

High-level view of completed SIPS construction project. (Courtesy of HOCA Practice, photo by author)

SIP manufacturers who provide a certified and approved system are usually circumspect as to their partnering relationship with contractors and insistent upon only providing their SIP building system to contractors who can demonstrate their skill in building with SIPS to an approved standard. As mentioned earlier, in the late 1940s SECO was one of the first prefabrication companies after the Second World War to engage in prefabricated building; they insisted on their partnering contractors undertaking the necessary training in order to complete the installation and erection process correctly. SIPS-accredited manufacturers maintain lists of approved place contractors who have been vetted and who can be recommended with confidence to clients and architects. The manufacturer's approved contractor functions as a partner with the manufacturer in delivering SIP buildings where the manufacturer delivers the fully certified building system as a kit of parts direct from the factory to the site for their approved contractor to construct. Clients are further protected as the same contractor is registered with an approval body which provides warranty and insurance, although an element of confusion prevails about what is meant by 'warranty' and 'guarantee' (see Chapter 7, 'Certified Approvals').

Whilst the assembly period on-site is relatively quicker than that associated with conventional construction, the exposure of the SIP's OSB skins, in particular during erection and until the superstructure assembly is completed, is an aspect which should not be ignored as leaving the SIP exposed for long periods should be avoided. The kit of parts consists primarily of standard panel widths of 1,220mm (see Chapter 4, 'Standardized Components and System Build') to lengths prescribed by the architect's fabrication design, with insulated splines and full timber splines, timber top and bottom rails, timber soleplates, fabricated lintels and any other associated components unique to the SIP system for the building. Buildings delivered in this way are usually applied to single houses or small housing projects and require a 'lead-in' and manufacturing time period of around six to eight weeks from the point of completing the architect's fabrication drawings to delivery on-site. With proper coordination this period is used by the contractor to prepare the site, install the below-ground services and complete the foundations and ground-floor concrete slab, if pre-assembled floor cassettes are not used for the ground floor. With the site and foundations ready in advance immediate erection of the SIPS building should commence so as to avoid unnecessary prolonged exposure of the panels.

Not all projects are procured in this way. There are occasions when standard 1,220mm-wide panels are delivered from the panel manufacturer to another factory to assemble complete walls to the lengths and heights prescribed by the architect. In addition, very often the floor and roof components for the project are assembled in this way, also thereby arriving at a

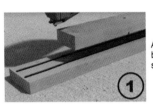

Assembling timber bottom rail to timber sole plate - 1

Securing bottom rail and sole plate to top of concrete slab foundation with damp proof layer under sole plate - 2

SIPS components and assembly process. (Courtesy of Kingspan TEK Building System)

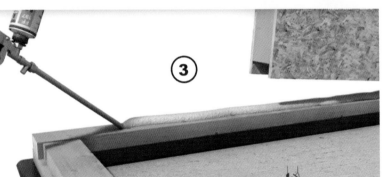

Preparing top of bottom rail to receive structural insulated panel (SIP) - 3

Insulated spline connection between panels nailed fixed on both sides - 1 and 2

Insulated spline

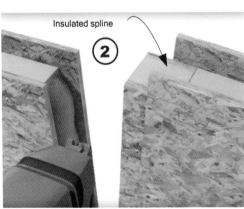

Connecting 1220mm standard width panels with insulated splines or timber splines to provide additional structural support within wall - 3

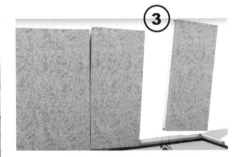

Panel-jointing connection for SIP building system. (Courtesy of Kingspan TEK Building System)

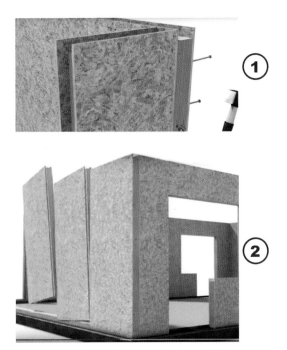

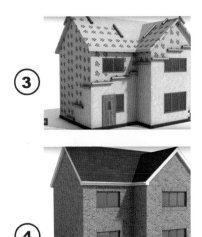

SIP building system: (1) corner connection; (2) return wall assembly; (3) breather membrane (wrap); (4) external brick cladding. (Courtesy of Kingspan TEK Building System)

situation where all wall sections together with floor and roof cassettes are delivered to the site in a completed state and ready for immediate installation on-site as opposed to assembling the kit of parts on-site. There are some advantages in this process as much of the wall, floor and roof assembly process is completed within the factory environment, which is an ideal situation, especially during the winter months. Completed wall sections delivered to the site can also include the external breather membrane and timber battens in readiness for the external cladding system. The external breather membrane also provides weather protection to the SIP wall panel. When brickwork is used externally there is no requirement

Panelized building with timber battens and specified screws fixed into 15mm-thick OSB TEK building system, ensuring no pull-out when final external metal cladding system is installed. (Photo by author)

for the timber battens as the breather membrane is staple-fixed to the face of the OSB. Internally, the finishing process is somewhat different; the decision on whether the finishes are factory-applied or applied on-site will dictate the best approach.

It is not necessary to apply a vapour control layer to the SIP wall internally; however, it is recognized as good practice in the UK to do so by installing a conventional polythene layer to the internal face of the SIP wall which is held in place by timber battens. The battens are normally 25mm thick and will form a service void behind the internal plasterboard lining. Applying a polythene vapour control layer as described will also provide protection to the SIP wall during transit to the site and while left exposed on the site for a period of time during installation and finishing. The polythene vapour control layer can be omitted and substituted by a foil-backed plasterboard lining but the weather protection to the SIP wall and roof is lost as a consequence if the same is applied as an on-site activity.

Where additional fire rating is required to the SIP wall a plasterboard layer of appropriate thickness is first applied to the inside face of the SIP's OSB skin, which could have a foil backing to facilitate vapour control if deemed necessary. The service void is then created by battening out over the first plasterboard layer and further plasterboard lining is applied to the

SIPS complete wall section under installation to top of timber bottom rail. (Courtesy of Kingspan Timber Solutions Ltd)

front of the timber battens for final finishing purposes, which may provide the required acoustic rating and additional fire protection. The architect is best placed to specify these materials and requirements to achieve the correct wall specifications irrespective of whether they are to function as external perimeter walls, internal compartment walls or internal partition walls.

As a building system SIPS is a very versatile method of construction. It is lightweight and yet for domestic and light commercial projects is capable of competing very favourably with conventional construction as well as with its immediate closed panel competitor. 'Build over' projects too are easily achieved with SIPS and it is often applicable where there is an opportunity to build on top of an existing building where additional space is at a premium. The most convenient building type is where an existing building has a flat roof, such as a school which is seeking additional classroom space but does not want to surrender valuable play space at ground level, or where owners of an apartment block want to create additional apartments, or indeed commercial buildings where additional space would facilitate business expansion.

Build over school project using SIPs with external cladding material. (Photo by author)

Panelization and Extent of Use

One of the fundamental attractions of panelized prefabrication is its light weight when compared to conventional construction. As such, it presents itself as an ideal choice for numerous building applications and community-size projects generally but housing in particular attracts significant attention. School building, too, is seen as a prime market for the manufacturer, where any space from single classrooms to a complete school is common in both SIP building systems and closed panel construction. Whilst four to six storeys in height is becoming commonplace for closed panel and SIP building projects, it is less so when compared to taller public buildings where significantly larger structural spans with open space are required and which are usually constructed using conventional construction processes. There are situations where a prefabricated building can commence from the top of an existing building as a build over: a prefabricated building is simply placed on a flat-roofed building. This option has already been explored for many years but of late prefabrication techniques have provided some very sophisticated design solutions.

Panelization presents a number of system options that are available, some with varying degrees of

Early build over project using panelized application set back from main elevation with rendered finish. (Photo by author)

completion at the time of leaving the factory and some more appropriate than others for particular applications. Within the UK there are three types of wall panels in common use for prefabricated buildings where each varies in appropriateness as to its ability to function effectively as part of an external wall without further supplementary work on-site by the contractor.

Open and Closed Panel Options

The open panel option is very limited in what it can achieve as a complete panelized component, given its raw state when dispatched to the site and the amount of work remaining to be completed by the contractor in order to render the panel component functional as a wall, whether internally or externally. On its own it is merely a number of timber studs held together by OSB sheathing, which is what it is meant to be. Consequently, the scope of applications for the open

panel as a complete entity are non-existent in that the outstanding work to be carried out by the contractor equates to almost a full conventional building project, thereby disqualifying the open panel work process from being described as prefabricated building.

The closed panel system takes panels to a more complete status at the point of leaving the factory and with significantly less work remaining for the contractor to complete on-site. Closed panels can be completed in the factory to a stage which incorporates the external breather membrane and only the external cladding system has to be completed. Similarly, the internal timber battening can be completed in the factory and be ready for the final layers of plasterboard linings which will be completed by the contractor on the site. There are, of course, other combinations and states of completion for the internal side of the closed panel: these are usually decided upon at the time of placing the order for the work.

It is worth noting the extent to which the closed panel option is completed. It should be dictated by

Closed panel installed as a fully completed wall panel section, with internal timber battens left ready to create services void and final plasterboard linings applications. (Courtesy of Kingspan Timber Solutions Ltd)

the architect but where this decision is left to the contractor (design and build), he/she may choose to have the panel only partially factory-completed, with first-fix electrics, internal battening, supplementary insulation and external battening excluded, almost to a point where it could not sensibly be referred to as a closed panel. By omitting these elements from the manufacturer's work package and completing them on-site, all associated costs and profit matters are therefore in the control of the contractor. The purpose of designing for manufacture and assembly is for the assembly work to be completed within the factory environment as much as possible, thereby ensuring greater quality control throughout and negating the inconsistencies of the on-site conditions. There are at least five of the six primary material elements (*see above*, bullet list under the heading 'Open Wall Panel Construction') which should be included as part of the panel manufacture and assembly process. The only remaining element is the control of water penetration, which can only be satisfied with the installation of the external cladding system on-site.

SIP Option and Modular Buildings

SIP is the third panel option which can be produced by a specialist manufacturing process and made available to the market as a kit of parts for a contractor to install on-site. SIP is a complete entity which is adopted by off-site manufacturers so as to create a wall panel that is used in panelized buildings. The raw structural insulated panel is manufactured in a standard width of 1.22m and maximum lengths of 6m and is then used to create wall panels in lengths prescribed by the architect's design. As with the closed panel, the structural insulated panel can also be assembled to a stage where five of the six primary material elements are completed within the factory with only the external cladding element remaining to be completed.

Whilst SIP is generally recognized as a panel system or building system employed in buildings at the site, there is also another application where it is used as wall panels in the assembly of volumetric modular units. Modular units manufactured in this way make efficient use of the characteristics of SIP by having a ready-made wall system at varying thicknesses available. When assembled with the floor and lid cassettes only the internal plasterboard linings and external cladding systems remain to be completed. It is an effective solution for single houses and housing projects of any number and for apartment buildings, usually up to four storeys high for accreditation purposes.

Wall Panel as Cladding and Structure

Not all building projects seek to employ timber floor and roof cassettes as the building design may dictate a preference for a different floor system to be used, such as precast concrete planks or beam and block solutions. Omitting timber floor and roof cassettes, however, and only using wall panels is not efficient and the validity of only using wall panels in isolation would have to be questioned as a prefabricated building design.

The case for PAMA lies solely in employing panelized prefabrication as a means for delivering the building's entire superstructure consisting of all walls, floors and roofs which are manufactured entirely within a factory environment. The concept for panelization, however, is that prefabricated panels are employed in a number of ways. Whilst the thermal properties for both panel types can be made to achieve the required values for a given situation, SIPS is more lightweight without losing its ability to perform structurally for four storeys in height to BBA certification. Apart from functioning as a substitute for conventional materials providing superior thermal performance or acting in a structural capacity or both, panelization is also employed by design as a primary external wall element; that is, the wall panel provides the external envelope to the building.

Prefabricated panels (that is, closed panels or SIPs employed in this way) are used in conjunction with the building's structural frame by mechanically fixing the panels to the external side of the structural frame, usually steel, as it is a complementary fast-track construction process. Used in this way they are not required to function as structural elements, but merely as a means to form the external perimeter walls of the building. Whilst fixed back to the structural frame of the building they can also provide their own self-support by the manner in which they are secured to the ground, usually by some simple fixing method. Selecting the type of wall panel is not too difficult: the idea is to focus on one which is lightweight and provides the appropriate thermal properties, satisfactory structural properties and the least amount of assembly. In this regard the structural insulated panel fulfils this criterion very well and is used successfully on numerous projects. (See Chapter 4, 'Customized Panelization'.)

Being a composite insulated panel system, SIPS panelization presents itself as very effective in addressing cold bridging as the structural frame is insulated and separated from the exterior. Placing the structural insulated panel on the external side of the structural frame allows for the maximum internal floor space to be created. Where the wall panel element is located within the frame zone two situations arise. First, the structural frame will have to be insulated in some way, thereby negating the benefit of using an insulated panel, and second, valuable floor space is surrendered.

Structural insulated panels employed in this way demonstrate the versatility of SIPS where the installation of maximum panel lengths on-site can achieve two-storey height for each panel. Moreover, being a composite insulated panel, both sides of the panel are ready for battening out immediately whereby both the internal first-fix electrics and plasterboard linings can commence and the installation of the external cladding system can progress to completion in parallel.

External Cladding

It is generally accepted that the final external cladding installation is an activity that can only sensibly be completed on-site, which is the ingredient missing from total factory prefabrication. External brick cladding is the most common choice within the UK, given its historic association over the centuries. Rendering is another attractive option for economic reasons whilst metal and tile cladding systems are also employed. The ability to remove this on-site fixing activity and incorporate the same as part of the overall panel manufacturing process within the factory environment is the preferred option but is limited to a very small number of manufacturers and for the process to be undertaken and completed to an acceptable standard and quality it requires specialized automated machinery which is not commonplace in the UK as yet.

Currently, once the selected panel solution has been installed the final external cladding system, often referred to as the building's envelope, can be applied immediately. There are numerous options used today, some of which include timber cladding, lead, zinc, copper and other metal sheet cladding materials, even lightweight decorative concrete panels which are fast becoming a realistic option for architects. Very often within the UK an external brick outer leaf is preferred for which an appropriate foundation will be required at ground level. Brickwork, too, can also commence from any of the upper floor levels but this would prove to be unnecessarily expensive, structurally challenging and questionable as to why timber wall panels are used in the building in the first place when a traditional build solution or precast concrete wall panels might be more appropriate. Maximum benefits and advantages are more easily realized when the maximum number of 'wet trades' are designed out and do not form part of the prefabricated architecture philosophy: in such cases there is tremendous scope for an efficient brick slip application process.

As with other sheet materials for external cladding, technological advances are being made in relation to brick slip applications as viable substitutes for traditional brickwork. Brick cladding in the form of brick slips is a popular option for many developers wishing to satisfying planning and fulfil their quest to honour traditional values and expectations. Where the architect designs in use of brick slips at the initial concept design stage they are usually best applied within the factory environment where the end result will prove more successful. The majority of panel manufacturers fail to provide a satisfactory result in applying brick slips, usually because it is executed by hand in the factory. So in practice, unless the manufacturer is fully automated with the machinery specifically designed to apply brick slips the architect would do well to consider an alternative external cladding regime. The architect would also do well to be forever mindful of the architectural detailing associated with joints and junctions which, for the architect skilled and experienced in manufacturing and assembly processes, lends opportunities for innovativeness and flair.

External metal cladding system and timber battens fixed to SIP building system using 15mm-thick OSB for structural and fixing purposes. (Photo by author)

Automation is recognized as the most satisfactory option for achieving precision and exactness when using brick slips in panelized and modular buildings. (Courtesy of JJ Smith & Co. (Woodworking Machinery) Ltd)

Stick-Build Construction

'Stick-built' is a term used, predominately in North America, to describe a method of timber construction carried out on-site in the UK where the labour skills of carpenters and joiners are employed by the main contractor, usually as a sub-contractor. In North America the specialist's sub-contractor is referred to as 'framing crew' who also possess similar work skills.

In the US and Canada 'stick-built' has long been seen as a traditional way for house construction but more recently is referred to as 'stick-built homes'

Typical stick-built construction, often referred to as 'timber-frame' building in the UK.

whilst in the UK this form of building first presented itself as a viable option for house building in the mid-1960s. It is often referred to as 'timber-framed construction', which is not necessarily the correct term, although the building does undergo a form of framing in the construction process on-site in order to make the building structurally stable. The word 'stick' refers to the pieces of timber that go into making the structure for the walls and roof, all of which is referred to as the 'superstructure'. Once the superstructure is completed the external cladding can be applied: this might consist of facing bricks or a proprietary timber or metal cladding rainscreen system. With the external cladding complete to provide weathertight conditions, the remainder of the internal fitting out and finishes can proceed under cover.

The stick-built method of construction means each and every piece of timber is treated as a separate component, a method which by its very nature is time-consuming. The pieces of timber arrive on-site in varying lengths, but the contractor would seek to source the timber in convenient lengths to build the house (or other building) according to the prescribed dimensions so as to minimize waste and reduce costs. Notwithstanding, the stick-built construction necessitates each piece of timber to be individually handled, measured and cut, then fitted and nailed into position, which, for even a modest size building project, can be a very time-consuming endeavour. There are clearly some significant disadvantages with this type of construction process, especially when dealing with UK weather conditions as delays can result unless this phase of the work is scheduled appropriately. Inclement weather can also affect the condition of the exposed timber to the extent that when it is subjected to the periods of wet or moist conditions the moisture retained in the timber can cause it to warp, become bent and twisted, impact on its structural effectiveness and be in an unsuitable state for applying the plasterboard systems internally or, indeed, the OSB or ply sheathing externally. The degree to which stick-built projects can be conveniently adjusted and even radically changed whilst under construction on-site is highlighted as a possible advantage and when compared to alternative options associated with OSM such as panelization or modularization a measure of validity exists.

A perception sometimes voiced is that stick-built houses are constructed in a superior way, but this would be subject to the standard of workmanship employed by the builder and the team of carpenters and joiners. Being such a personalized venture, the builder retains absolute control of the work as it progresses on-site from ordering materials to assembling the timber superstructure on-site. Compared to a prefabricated solution the suggestion put forward is that the stick-built building will have a longer life span and present itself as having superior resale value. There is no clear data readily available from detailed analysis to confirm this one way or the other. Time and cost comparisons between traditional stick-built construction and factory-produced panelized or modular alternative solutions are not clear and definitive enough to identify an absolute difference, as aspects relating to procurement and delivery methods are radically different. What is clear, however, is that the less time the contractor is on the site the more efficient the build process will be as a result, and because of this, costs and quality are affected accordingly. Notably, as stick-build on-site may take many weeks of construction to achieve weathertight conditions it is therefore unable to compete with the speed at which a full closed panel can deliver the same objective as measured in mere days or with modular building which requires even fewer days for assembly at the site.

There are many houses today still constructed using this technique, but it tends to be more popular with the smaller builder engaged on smaller projects where housing is the focus. Current trends, however, indicate a move away from the labour-intensive activities associated with stick-built on-site, even for the small builder, as much of the timber assembly work can be undertaken within a factory environment employing technological advances that eliminate time and costs associated with all the on-site measuring, cutting, hammering and nail-banging whilst at the same time introducing improved levels of accuracy and quality. In essence, the factory intervention transforms the on-site stick-built concept into panelized products where timber panels are assembled into frame units to prescribed length and height, with both sides open but temporarily wrapped in a protective material for transportation and installation purposes. This is a form of timber frame construction which realistically, however, is just one level above on-site stick-built construction process. It can demonstrate itself to be a more economical alternative in terms of operatives' time on-site and lost time due to inclement weather; it also reduces the risk of fire, negates the potential for timber warping and twisting and can be enclosed more expeditiously, both externally and internally.

Precast Concrete Panels

Precast concrete panels have a history dating back to around 1905 when an engineer from Liverpool named John Brodie developed precast panelled buildings. The concept of concrete panelization instilled the notion of industrialization and standardization in building. As noted earlier, in the UK this concept was cradled by the Industrial Revolution but it gathered much greater momentum in the socialist economies of Eastern Europe following World War Two.

For many the perception associated with prefabricated concrete panels is one of images synonymous with high-rise apartment block housing predominately in many of the Eastern Bloc countries, although numerous examples presented themselves within the UK too. Across socialist and non-socialist Europe, including the UK, millions of homes had to be constructed following the destruction and devastation resulting from six years of war. From 1948 until the late 1980s when the communist regimes in Europe began to crumble, state-organized construction programmes produced many thousands of monumental free-standing apartment blocks where standardized prefabricated concrete panels were relied upon as a means for delivering fast-track construction. In the UK too, mass-produced housing was perceived at

Ubiquitous concrete panel construction.

the time as the ultimate solution, and whilst many variations of prefabricated housing were employed to solve the housing shortage (including precast concrete panels), it did not address the chronic demand which prevailed in the country after the war.

From the end of World War Two until the late 1980s the concept of prefabricated concrete panels production and its resulting architecture evolved to a much larger extent within the continent of Europe. The 'tower block' as it is referred to in the UK was synonymous with a lasting image impressed in the minds of many. However, unlike communist Europe, the tower block ideal in the UK did not survive as long until the late 1980s.

Unlike the prefabricated single-storey timber bungalow, concrete panelization in particular had the ability to create high-rise buildings and presented itself as an obvious option for managing the acute housing shortage on a mass scale following the Second World War. The concept for precast concrete panels known as large panel system (LPS) embraced walls and floors to provide a total panelized system. It was assembled on-site in a cross-wall construction method, like a 'house of cards', and was dependent upon its own weight and a joint system referred to in later reports as the H-2 joint. Apartments and high-rise are perfect companions in terms of multi-repetition and standardization but by the time the report on Ronan Point was finally published six months after the disaster, twice as many LPS tower blocks had been completed as had stood on 16 May (*see below*).

The demand for mass-produced housing in the late 1950s, through all of the 1960s and into the beginning of the 1970s in the UK brought with it a mass-produced solution where standard reusable moulds produced standard panels more economically and more expeditiously. The result led to a boom in high-rise tower blocks in the 1960s which, for many, represented the epitome of visually drab and boring buildings, devoid of any real or familiar environmental context; these were depressing unsocial places to live in and were divorced from

the physical connection with ground level which had hitherto allowed communities to function and flourish as had been the situation for many previous generations. Such was the urgency for housing that social engineering was fused with industrial engineering more than promoting architect design solutions. Or was it that architects failed to recognize the design opportunities?

On 16 May 1968 at 5.45am, however, a significant event happened. At Ronan Point, a twenty-two-storey tower block located in the Borough of Newham, East London, and occupied for just two months by residents, became known for all the wrong reasons. A small gas explosion caused walls to blow out, resulting in the total collapse of one corner of the building. This incident not only challenged prefabricated concrete panels as a method of construction

Ronan Point, showing large panel construction.

but also the reputation of the architectural profession. Modernism, too, and its association with the tower blocks and prefabricated high-rise symbolized by the concrete panel in particular was also subject to equal criticism. Following the Ronan Point tragedy, the ability to justify solving housing shortages using prefabricated concrete panel construction methods began to wane at a rapid pace. Indeed, the concept of mass housing in tower blocks lost its appeal, more for social reasons than the effectiveness of the structural techniques, to the extent that some local authority architects opted not to engage in the design process of forty-storey tower blocks under feasibility design within the London Borough of Lambeth in the early 1970s. Ronan Point itself was demolished in 1984, with all of the nine tower blocks cleared in 1986 in readiness for a redevelopment to consist of two-storey houses with gardens. Reconnecting families with the ground level was considered the correct policy and a means to stimulate communities again.

The precast concrete panel has not gone away. In fact, there is a new resurgence in the use of prefabricated concrete panels and a new architecture evolving as a consequence where some architects recognize the attributes that prefabrication of this nature can bring to a project. Speed of installation, acoustic versatility, robustness, fireproofing capabilities, durability, thermal efficiency, weatherproofing and low maintenance represent some of the principal attributes associated with concrete panels. More significant, perhaps, is that the precast concrete panel is far more versatile than its predecessor of the 1950s and 1960s where standardization took precedent over architectural design. Moulds today are more obliging as they

New architect design approach in concrete panels: one available textured finish.

Alternative
textured panel
finish in concrete.

can be designed to be customized to replicate shapes and forms and simulate other materials and patterns, allowing the architect considerable scope and potential to make the external treatment of the building fit in with the existing environmental context or be an architectural expression in its own right. In today's UK market, prefabricated concrete panels compete well with current alternative methods of construction and are often used in conjunction with steel frame where speed of construction is paramount.

Larger and taller public and commercial buildings tend to be likely candidates for prefabricated concrete panels but as yet there appears to be less of an appetite for small-scale housing and residential projects where open and closed timber panel and SIP building systems solutions dominate. The technology employed in prefabricated concrete today allows the architect to design with an unlimited range of options to satisfy human scale and visual aesthetics, irrespective of whether it refers to historic stone reference, brick façades or modern art. The capacity for manufacturers to produce prefabricated concrete panels with precision and exactness is real as is the

Cast-in brick
slip facing as a
composite panel
solution. (Photos
by author)

ability to deliver high-quality textures, some of which include exposed-aggregate finishes, sand-blasting, honing or polished finishes and numerous other alternatives. In many situations architectural concrete is a modern solution, whether employed for civil engineering, economic or aesthetic reasons. Visual concrete relates to public buildings such as museums, concert halls, university buildings and stadiums and in the specialist-designed home too, where expressions of minimalism are clearly in evidence. The scope for prefabricated concrete panels to expand in the domestic market is reflected by the enquiries expressed, albeit at a slow pace. Expressions of interest are sought more by developers, builders and clients who seek to secure cost- and time-efficiencies as well as expand architectural design beyond the traditional.

Chapter Six

Prefabrication Through Premanufactured Volumetric Modular

Introduction

For more than twenty years the resurgence of interest in modular buildings has become something more than merely a reinvention of manufacturing techniques inherited from the early and mid-1960s when it was so urgent to find a solution to the housing shortage of the time. The thrust behind prefabricated and modular buildings today might still have a similar degree of urgency but not all for the same reasons. Indeed, there is still a shortage of housing but more specific to PAMA objectives is the latter's potential for affordability, somewhat beyond the reach of many through conventional construction, and architectural design which until relatively recently appeared not to have a place at all in the manufacture of prefabricated buildings.

The challenge enveloping PAMA and modular buildings in particular for most clients and government procurement officials is to test its ability to deliver an alternative to conventional construction at a more affordable cost or to achieve more building for the same cost or even less. The mechanics for creating a new order in modular architecture

Modular living: a new perception in modular accommodation. (Photo by author)

is often seen as a task for the manufacturer, where a notion of industrialized construction is seen as the vehicle for satisfying the brief as the sole objective, assisted by standardization but not necessarily under the design direction of the architect. The distinctiveness of every building or group of buildings, however, is the architectural intelligence associated with individuality where design principles and the resulting aesthetic is a natural outcome of the design process.

Beyond the ability to manufacture in a competent and effective manner lies the challenge for architects in the evolution of architectural design for modular buildings through artificial intelligence (AI). There is no certainty yet how the architectural design profession will adopt robotic involvement or to what extent AI in robots will be involved in architectural design processes of the future. However, if a new industrial revolution is to occur, which is very likely, architects should focus on ensuring they are instrumental in producing and organizing the array of design data required for robot production lest the robots are designed to undertake the task themselves.

The Modular Build Phenomenon

The word 'module' can be traced back to the sixteenth and seventeenth centuries, for which period the *Oxford English Dictionary* shows it overlapping substantially with 'model' in the sense of either a small-scale representation or as an example to follow (*see* Chapter 1, 'Core Elements Defining Prefabrication'). Not until the mid-eighteenth century did the notion of modularity present itself as we identify it today but more under the guise of industrialization and standardization and not necessarily as an architectural design concept. Modularity in architectural design refers to a module which for the greater part of the twentieth century was an autonomous component of design, an entity of manufacture reproduction to a standard size (Salingaros, 2008). What is perceived to be accepted as modularity in architectural literature is that which has a focus on 'modules and modular systems in design and construction' but which is not necessarily true in actuality, where architectural design is absent for much of the manufacturing process. Standardized products were

New heights for modular buildings. (Courtesy of CIMC MBS Ltd)

manufactured to a unified measurement which led to unified parts being used as a construction process. For the early industrialist, there was a natural transition from manufacturing standardized common parts and components to erecting common unified buildings, culminating ultimately in the concept of unitized building where each living unit or apartment was common or the same and the construction method founded on panelization.

Unitized construction is synonymous with prefabricated panels (panelization) and in today's context is associated with conventional construction projects where repetition of the panel unit or component is represented. The concept of unitized building can also apply to three-dimensional volumetric modular units where each modular unit can function as one separate building or when a number of units are assembled together to form a complete modular building assemblage. The difference here, however, is the fact that a modular building results from modular units that are premanufactured in a factory as a completed entity, as opposed to a unitized building which is derived from a panelized construction process on-site.

In architecture and building, concepts surrounding unitized buildings of earlier decades evolved from the efficiencies afforded through standardization in manufacturing but that too was more for the purpose of manufacturing expediency and cost-efficiencies in erecting buildings rather than seeking to foster an architectural design philosophy founded on modularization. Paxton's Crystal Palace may have been instrumental in introducing modular concepts founded on standardized industrialization and assembly techniques; conventional construction, however, has for a number of generations since employed modularity in unitized façades and geometric form where the building's architecture seeks to express the same. Currently, the word 'modular' is often interpreted in two ways: firstly, as an entity applied to buildings where they consist of factory-produced panelized components only and form a part of the conventional construction process or, secondly, as completed premanufactured assembly such as modular units as identified today which represent a more accurate terminology within which 'modular' is characterized as a PAMA concept.

Commercial office building with modular glass façade.

Glass façade with modular geometry: an office building on Wilhelmstrasse 65 in Berlin-Mitte belonging to the German parliament.

Standardized octagonal and cuboidal modular unit arrangement designed to create a complete primary school. (Courtesy of HOCA Practice)

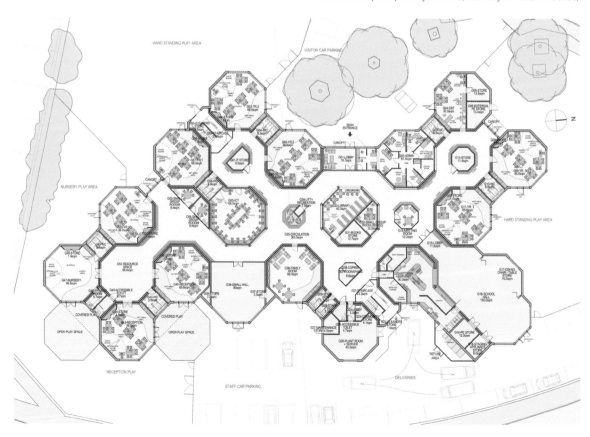

Interconnecting octagonal and cuboidal teaching spaces for new primary school. (Courtesy of HOCA Practice)

Premanufactured Modular Buildings

Standardized Multi-Purpose Buildings

It would be reasonable to suggest that in too many instances the end result for a standardized modular build project is disappointing, where the finished product fails to meet expectations either visually or in suitability for a given site context. Standardized modular buildings that depict historic perceptions associated with prefabrication usually revolve around the concept of a ready-made modular unit which is a pre-designed mass-produced entity, enabling an instant ready-made building solution that can be delivered to a site location immediately and erected in days. Concerns and observations such as these may be justified for a number of reasons. Little if any expertise of a trained architect forms any part of the overall design and manufacturing process and may be seen as irrelevant, as the said buildings are made to satisfy particular markets where transience has precedence over longevity. Indeed, much of what

Historic perceptions of modular building reinforced by temporary school classrooms which have survived generations of schoolchildren. (Photo by author)

Current modular temporary classrooms in common use. (Photo by author)

as the concept that lies behind employing ready-made modular buildings is that one type fits all, like a unitized solution, which is not what architecture is meant to represent, given its relationship to a specific site context, functionality and architectural reference, all of which are unique to each site location. This is not to suggest, however, the same manufacturing and assembly technology, coupled with the skills, knowledge, expertise and experience of the factory, cannot be employed repeatedly in the architectural design of premanufactured modular buildings instead. However, the uniqueness of every project, its architectural principles and aesthetic, its justification for occupying a space within the urban or rural environment in the first place can only be sensibly and sensitively handled under the direction of trained architects. History has already demonstrated the results of the early and mid-twentieth century when prefabricated architecture primarily consisted of a manufacturing process as opposed to a design-led enterprise, the results of which continue to transmit negative perceptions.

Modular Design and Current Trends

Whilst historically, prefabrication has always had an emphasis on housing, and in some instances has been a means of satisfying urgent housing requirements, current UK trends are now focusing on building projects other than residential ones alone. Residential and family housing remain the primary market in the UK for PAMA where apartment blocks of varying storey heights are prime candidates, given the almost infinite plan layout arrangements available, current levels of manufacturing technology and rapid on-site assembly process available. Two-, three- and four-storey houses, where each floor level consists of one complete module, also have a particular focus and continue to remain a preferred option for addressing the current UK housing shortage but will only have real success where government promotes some measure of volume production on a consistent basis.

ready-made buildings represent in terms of build quality or, indeed, aesthetic value is reflected in the repetitive form and materials used.

Buildings procured through a ready-made system route can be identified as pure building exercises, as the degree to which any architecture is represented (if at all) is expressed by automatic default given the manner in which the building was considered; in other words, the economics associated with basic material selection, rapid fabrication and express installation are evident. The resulting architecture, therefore, is by default and less by design,

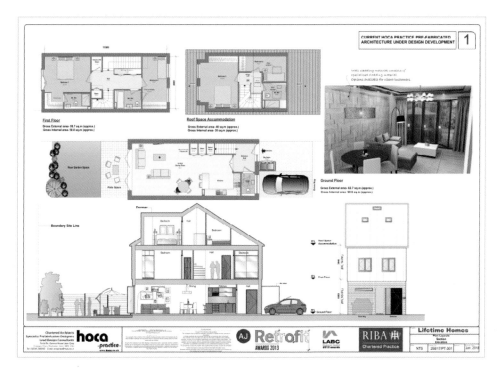

Premanufactured modular eco-house design for the Lifetime Home solutions where each floor level is a separate modular unit. (Courtesy of HOCA Practice)

Interior of premanufactured modular Lifetime Home, promoting superior quality space and interior finishes. (Courtesy of HOCA Practice)

Modular buildings satisfy expectations when applied to controlled manufacturing and assembly, speed of final assembly at the site and project cost-effectiveness as well as delivering quality architectural detailing and finishes in conjunction with precision and exactness, all of which form the very essence of PAMA. There are numerous examples of modular buildings, ranging through complete schools, community buildings, sports and recreation facilities, hotel rooms, complete bathroom modules and student sleeping/study modules.

In more recent years significant strides have been made in highlighting many of the attributes, advantages and benefits associated with modular buildings and, with many successful projects completed in a number of sectors, their validity and viability is clearly demonstrated. The emphasis now should be focused on developing PAMA to the next level in terms of architectural design allied to manufacturing and assembly advancement as a joined-up exercise in one seamless enterprise. However, some might argue there are more constraints within the manufacturing

New prefabricated sports club facilities building using SIPs with timber, metal and render external cladding. (Courtesy of HOCA Practice)

Space-saving solution with build over school project on top of existing school hall, using closed panel construction with external rendering to create additional teaching spaces. (Photo by author)

Build-Over in-fill school project in prefabricated architecture allows valuable roof space to be created over an existing school hall roof

Lightweight panelised construction creates additional teaching spaces without having to surrender valuable play space at ground level

Large open space using steel-framed modular units where each modular unit can be up to 27.4m long and 5.0m wide. (Photo by author)

Modular architecture and interiors: hotel bathroom. (Photo by author)

Modular architecture and interiors: hotel bedroom. Prefabricated and modular architecture delivers the repeated and consistent precision and exactness demanded for five-star hotel and living accommodation projects.

process and sufficient reason to abandon prefabrication as a viable alternative when compared with the conventional build process. This is a common view held mainly by those who seek to deliver buildings through conventional construction processes only. Where the trained architect is undertaking the lead consultant role in designing for manufacturing and assembly the attributes far outweigh constraints. Moreover, the contractual and management aspects associated with PAMA projects are not dissimilar to that of the conventional alternative which for the trained architect cancels out suggestions of unnecessary complications and difficulties.

The biggest fear doubters might have, however, is the notion of entrusting the whole of the superstructure for a modular building to a factory business which will remain beyond the comprehension of some. The perception of 'gamble' and 'risk' for others tends to be uppermost in the thinking of those functioning at project procurement and decision-making levels. For others who are perhaps more committed to conventional build practices only, there might also

appear to be good reason not to source a verified and established alternative because of diminished profit. The George Street project in Croydon in the UK by Tide Construction in conjunction with Vision Modular Systems places some of the negative perceptions into context with the near-completion of the world's tallest modular apartment building which is indicative of the PAMA philosophy. Whilst this new modular building is indicative of the modular building objective, in many respects it nonetheless relies on completing the building's façade with an on-site installation process as opposed to the preferred factory-applied process.

Premanufactured modular buildings are purposeful by their design intent specific to each building project where high design standards under the direction of the trained architect, knowledgeable and skilled in designing for manufacture and assembly, are the norm. Hotel projects are a specific case in point where high design standards, precision and superior quality are prerequisites. They are indicative of the high design standards and performance achievable

Modular hotel at Bristol Airport. (Photo by author)

through PAMA for sectors referred to earlier, thereby dispelling myths and perceptions usually attributed to prefabrication by those with a traditional agenda. The notion that all modular buildings continue to generate perceptions of a predictable rectangular box, suitable only for a multiplicity of small-scale ready-made or temporary applications, does not reflect the actuality of architectural design and manufacturing ingenuity which prevail today in terms of delivering completed modular buildings.

PAMA represents a distinctive philosophy for modular buildings in that its architectural design is architect-led; it is bound up with the specifics surrounding site context, functionality, architectural form and the precision of manufacturing and assembly technologies, all of which reside under the auspices of this new science of building. There are well-grounded and logical reasons, therefore, for clients and architects to rethink the manner in which their development site is managed in a global sense. PAMA is clear in its objective too. With the entire superstructure evolving from the factory environment followed by the manufacturer's assembly process at the site, the question now being asked is when the conventional term 'construction site' will cease to exist as an entity and the word 'construction'

substituted accordingly. Perhaps construction which is already referred to as industrialized construction in relation to modular buildings can now evolve into PAMA where architectural design has a central role.

General Characteristics

Modular buildings and modular homes have always appeared to be synonymous, although there are also examples of modular buildings that are factory-produced for other sectors too. The term 'modular' has a long association with prefabrication and system buildings where aspects of factory building, mass-production and standardization highlight some of the typical characteristics that remain omnipresent in the minds of many, even within the current context of PAMA. As noted under the heading 'Core Elements Defining Prefabrication and Modularization' in Chapter 1, there is a clear distinction between the on-site activities associated with conventional 'modular building' or 'modular construction' as opposed to a premanufactured 'modular building', which is an end product derived from an assembly process within a factory. The only element of the building's superstructure that has any relationship

Premanufactured modular family houses: each floor level is a separate modular unit fitted out at the factory before dispatch to the site location for final assembly. (Photo by author)

with the actual site, therefore, is at the time when the modular units are assembled together at the site to form the complete modular assemblage. Indeed, this final assembly process does not require skills normally associated with conventional construction as the complete building's assemblage is carried out by the manufacturer and not the contractor.

The common denominator that might continue to validate any relationship of 'modular building' or 'construction' as an on-site process is the interface between factory and site and this has a very limited extent in the context of modular buildings. The interface is the activity that takes place between the manufacturing process and the completed modular assemblage at the site location. It constitutes a measure of on-site work referred to as 'enabling works' for the modular units to be assembled into a modular superstructure. Many modular buildings are commissioned as self-supporting single-storey buildings; those of two and sometimes three or four storeys high are not uncommon. The nature and extent of the interface in this instance is limited whereby the enabling work required above ground for the modular superstructure is minimal and limited to the top of the foundations or the installation of a concrete slab upon which the modular units are to be fixed. The interface, then, is the connection between the factory assembly process and any enabling work required for the purpose of completing the modular assemblage at the site location.

Modular buildings are now becoming taller and, depending on the height of the modular building being proposed, the central core areas might be constructed as a reinforced concrete structure. The higher the building the greater the justification for such a solution, as a solid core of this nature provides the strong central spine around which the modular assemblage is arranged and to which it is anchored. The two modular towers for the world's tallest modular tower building in Croydon mentioned above are forty-four and thirty-six storeys high respectively and each has a reinforced concrete central core which accommodates the vertical circulation from ground

to roof level. Work on the two concrete central cores commenced on-site immediately following the completion of the foundations and the below-ground services installations; thus there was a smooth and brief interface between the production of the modular units within the factory and their final assembly at the site.

As with any building, vertical circulation routes are required for the full height of the building and their size and the most efficient location will depend on the building's intended use, its plan arrangement and its floor area at each level. Vertical circulation routes are catered for by way of central core areas within which stairs, lifts if required, electrical cupboards, storage and the like are located at each floor level; this is typical for apartment buildings. Within non-residential buildings, such as offices for instance, the central core will also accommodate toilets and activities which are common for the function and utilization of the building. The actual size of each floor area will dictate the number of stairs cores that will be required to render the building compliant in terms of functionality, travel distance and fire escape purposes.

Modular buildings are no different and the same rules and regulations apply. The plan form of the building is, however, defined more by the size of the modular units or modules which, when put together, result in a finished assemblage referred to as the modular building. For non-residential buildings the size of the standard modular unit forming the total assemblage will dictate what can be accommodated within each module forming the core areas. Some modular buildings will necessitate a number of modular units for the core areas in order for all of the common activities to be accommodated. Core areas are not necessarily located in the centre of the building; location at each end of the building is a common practice so as to adhere to the building control and means of escape requirements.

The thrust behind the design and production of premanufactured modular buildings in the UK continues to grow, albeit at a slow pace over the past two decades. Technology has coupled with a measure

Internal stairs within a single modular unit for the full height of the building and forming part of a central core. (Photo by author)

of design ingenuity to create a roadmap that takes modular buildings to new heights, forty and more storeys high in some cases. High-rise modular buildings are now possible where the structural integrity of the building is derived from the modular units themselves through the design and manufacturing process where the lower-level modular units have the structural capacity to support the modular units above. Within a high-rise modular building the thickness of the walls would naturally be thicker at the lower levels and reduce in thickness as the building increases in height, thereby allowing some additional space to be created within the upper-level modular units. This approach to designing high-rise modular buildings eliminates the need for any secondary structural support such as steel framing and reduces a high degree of enabling work at the site.

Design options associated with modular buildings are currently enjoying a renaissance where perceptions previously held about PAMA are under serious review. It is already demonstrated that modular units can be assembled and totally fitted out internally within the factory environment and delivered for their final assembly at the site. Consequently, the notion of industrialized construction in the UK is rapidly becoming a realization which brings premanufactured modular architecture into clearer focus for providing architectural design solutions and a certain reality for architects to recognize. Total PAMA, however, will not be achieved until the total completion of the external cladding treatment forms part of the factory process but this has not yet been brought to a satisfactory level of design and precision. The confidence attached to existing external cladding solutions has not yet risen to the point where a measure of perfection or acceptance is achieved to satisfy the aspirations of most architects. Further research and design development is necessary by architects in particular if this final challenge is to be accomplished.

Beyond Premanufactured Modular

Community buildings and social housing projects are forever seeking to achieve improved economies and whilst the notion of 'lean construction' has already been well tested to the point of exhaustion the universal

Machine automation providing factory 'hand-built' manufacturing and assembly. (Courtesy of Frame Homes (SW) Ltd)

emphasis now is to focus on greater efficiencies. Construction and prefabrication have always been closely associated but in reality the prefabricated elements have more to do with innovative fabrication design and manufacturing ingenuity. As manufacturing technology and automation become more omnipresent many different types of building in numerous sectors present themselves as viable candidates for modular buildings as a solution. The potential for achieving greater cost certainty and more predictable delivery dates is more easily achievable when the superstructure is premanufactured totally within a factory environment. The most powerful influencers and catalysts for adopting premanufactured modular buildings are standardization, repetition and volume, from which all the attributes associated with modularization are derived but without needing to abandon innovativeness and flexibility in architectural design. In other words, it is incumbent on the architect to adopt standardization of manufacturing without standardizing architectural design. The opportunities that prevail in modern automated manufacturing technology should act as a catalyst for architects to become more innovative in creating design options and alternatives for the next generation of modular buildings and thereby remain relevant for current and future prospects.

Housing in particular is synonymous with prefabrication (although it has impacted on many other sectors too) so it is not a new concept. The history surrounding modular residential buildings is well documented, as indeed are the sentiments and perceptions held by many over the past decades. However, premanufactured modular buildings have a new impetus and energy where automation and robotics are considered to be the key features in delivering modular buildings for the future. The ability to deliver completely fitted-out modules within a factory environment that are then finally assembled together at the site location is a major change of mindset for many within the construction industry. The notion of manufacturing houses, schools, health care builds and similar community buildings in a culture akin to the motor manufacturing industry is, for some, not necessarily unthinkable but probably impractical, unrealizable and even unworkable notwithstanding the same is already envisaged and the science and research already under way. Whilst the UK is perhaps a distance away from absorbing the concept of producing houses with 3D printing the technology does exist for this to happen but not to the point where houses can be rolled out for human habitation.

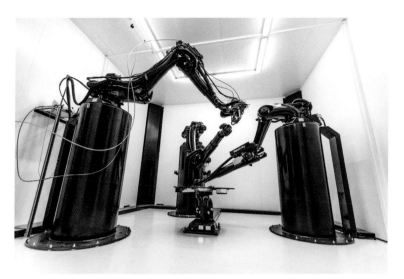

Advances in technology demonstrated by 3D metal printing of structures for rockets.

3D printed rocket, built for the University of Alberta Science Hackerspace.

For now, the possibility of the wider manufacturing fraternity taking over the production of most buildings currently exists, but within the current UK regime for delivering buildings, manufacturers' ability, knowledge and expertise to undertake and run an efficient turnkey project on-site from concept design to hand-over appears not to be their particular reason to exist nor indeed their preference, for now perhaps. In some instances, however, manufacturers might undertake specialist turnkey projects in order to remain relevant and in business. Equally, the reluctance of personnel within the conventional construction industry to fully engage with premanufactured modular buildings today has been highlighted for a number of specific reasons. With the advent of three-dimensional (3D) printed buildings it might not be possible to comprehend the level of fallout and catastrophe that will ensue when construction companies are faced with the reality of 'downing tools' totally, but for some, perhaps, they are already alert to this prospect by becoming industrialists themselves.

The next horizon is suggested as 3D printed architecture: there could be a further evolution in prefabricated and modular architecture where the current new science of premanufacturing modular

Hand-built craftsmanship, where William Morris believed the art of architecture should reside.

Modular unit produced with 3D printing, indicating the direction of travel for future modular architecture.

buildings through automation and robotics is perhaps superseded by 3D printed architecture. When the precision and exactness currently available through automation and robotics is advanced to new levels, it may have overtones of science fiction but, when 3D printed metal rocket parts are scheduled to journey into space and beyond, the notion of fiction is somewhat obsolete if not eliminated.

Most prototypes and research in 3D printed houses is limited to single-storey buildings. Up to very recently, however, modular buildings were also restricted in height but, as with any good idea, the engineering and the science will follow: we have already noted how its architectural design has resulted in a new forty-storey modular building at Croydon. It is not unreasonable, therefore, to believe the same will transpire with 3D printed buildings, where a new architecture with its new aesthetic might occupy our rural, urban and city environments in a new art of architecture. If the procurement processes for modular buildings on their own are possibly beyond acceptance for so many, is it possible to ever comprehend acceptance of 3D printed buildings and will it be left to science, research engineers and manufacturers, with architects observing from the sidelines? Just how relevant will architects and construction professionals be twenty years from now?

Automation, Robotics and Artificial Intelligence

The present status of premanufactured modular building is in a period of transition in its relationship with machine technology. It is necessary, therefore, to examine the practices of the past and the tools that were available to facilitate factory production up to the present. In reality, the majority of premanufactured modular buildings in the UK continue to be more 'hand-built', albeit in a factory environment and with some semblance of assembly line production. The principal ingredient continues to be the employment of skilled trades personnel, many of whom originate from conventional construction activities: electricians, plumbers, fitters of many types, roofers and the like.

There are distinct differences that exist for manufacturers and their skilled tradespeople too who opt to work within a factory as opposed to a conventional construction site. A primary feature is that a factory offers continuity in work-flow unaffected by inclement weather, which is an attraction for clients seeking to achieve certainty on completion dates, as well as negating possible contractor claims of delay through inclement weather. The manufacturer, too, has the ability to plan and forecast work-flow delivery dates with a greater measure of accuracy together with the facility to produce better quality and more precise workmanship: this certainly gives a clear advantage

over the on-site alternative. Even with this massive leap in attitudes and changed mindset, the production of the factory environment will soon come under a new wave of pressure for more productivity, more improved quality, precision and exactness, but with less human involvement in the actual assembly process.

For many manufacturers of modular buildings, the ambition might be to abandon the hand-built practices but where a skilled labour force is plentiful automation tends not to be urgent or an attractive proposition. For other manufacturers, however, automation is a necessary step where efficiencies of many descriptions are significant considerations irrespective of any robotic assembly element that could be included. The fact of the matter is that robotic assembly is merely a further evolution in automation (albeit with a bigger capital investment) which eliminates dependency on the 'hand-built' element. The motor industry is already committed to robotic assembly and car manufacturing robots certainly provide an increased competitive advantage. It is known that robotics in motor manufacturing delivers improved quality, increases capacity and at the same time provides the ability to design out bottlenecks. Equally significant is the environment within which workers can operate: safety and cleanliness prevail as does protection from dangerous and difficult activities. Whilst it is recognized that the activities associated with a motor manufacturing plant differ greatly from manufacturing modular buildings, in reality they both produce an end product. The scope for the enlightened modular building industrialist to adopt and incorporate automation with robotic assembly into future modular building manufacture is a brave leap indeed. Commitment to efficiency in production, however, can be easily measured against the attributes and benefits gained by the motor manufacturing industrialist.

CAD Technology

For hundreds of years until the late twentieth century the image of an architect at work was usually one

Architects using traditional drawing boards and T-squares at work on the new building programme in Washington DC, circa 1938.

which included the ubiquitous drawing board and T-square as a necessary set of tools in the practice of the profession. Generations of architects designed and detailed buildings with a love and passion where each separate drawing as it evolved from the drawing board became a personal work of art by the individual architect. Line differentiation was a keen feature by which to distinguish between presentation drawings and detailed working (construction) drawings where plans and cross-sections were subjected to the weight of the pencil lead on the paper, such was the artistry of the architect's drawings. A good set of hand-produced drawings would represent the architect's style which, within the profession, would identify its author to work colleagues like a set of fingerprints.

By the early 1980s computer aided design (CAD) presented itself to architects as a viable alternative to the approach of hand-drawing with drawing board and T-square, a skill which had existed for centuries previously. The response by many traditionalists within design fraternities was somewhat unfavourable, if not hostile towards a new technology that was perceived to threaten traditional methods and jobs. The perception was that architecture produced through CAD would merely result in a series of squares and rectangles, unlike the capacity of the individual architect producing traditional paper sketches, such was the belief surrounding the limitation of the computer. It was, however, quickly recognized that architects were being provided with a tool which generated greater flexibility in design; the ability to explore many different design options in a much shorter time tended to transform hostile attitudes into more accepting and committed engagement. The efficiencies with which CAD now empowers architects in the production of architectural design through to three-dimensional construction detail drawings for building projects are in essence transformational and revolutionary.

The integration of CAD as a feature of the manufacturing world has a history dating back to the later 1950s but it was not until 1984 that a division within

Hewlett-Packard established a mission to develop CAD and computer aided manufacturing (CAM) as an integrated software where CAD creates the design and CAM builds it in a seamless operation. Integrated CAD/CAM software is a combined endeavour where the CAD element produces output in the form of a 2D drawing or a 3D model CAD file suitable to be imported into the CAM software which ultimately manufactures the end product.

CAD/CAM and BIM

In architectural practice the concept of CAD/CAM became a feature of building information modelling (BIM) where 3D design and modelling of the building's architecture provide architects with the tools to plan and design as well as construct and manage the overall delivery processes for buildings in collaboration with other design and construction professionals. In essence BIM represents the building's physical and functional characteristics and provides the design team with the opportunity to interact during all the design stages, where the structural engineer can input his/her structural design into the architect's concept development as indeed can the building services engineer. Every component of the building, such as a door, a window, a wall type, a lift, an HVAC system, a material used in the building's design, is essentially a BIM object with a high level of product information attached to it. The data file informs design and construction professionals as to the properties of each of the building's products (such as thermal performance or physical characteristics). It thus provides an on-screen graphical representation of what the product looks like and the product's functional data, allowing users to manipulate the object in the way it is intended to be used. This hitherto applied to conventional building practices but now includes

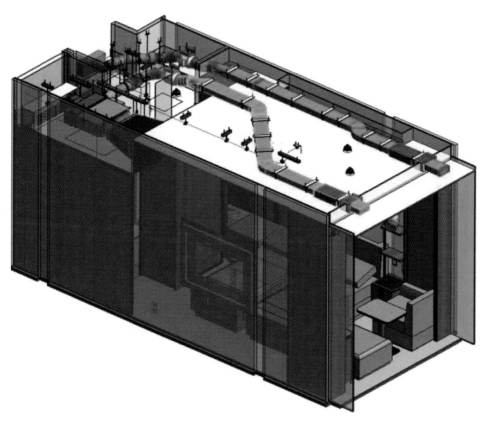

This CAD drawing shows typical input by architect and services engineer for a hotel modular unit as part of factory production. (Courtesy of CIMC MBS Ltd)

modular buildings, with even greater impact. With the ability of the designers to manipulate, test and interrogate all design disciplines, the potential for any possible 'clash' is identified at the early stages of the design process, thereby allowing for more accurate costing and scheduling.

Computer aided engineering (CAE) software is also making a significant contribution to the design of buildings recently by being able to (for example) predict wind loads on buildings and the impact on pedestrians at ground level in urban areas, control air quality, validate HVAC systems, predict the spread of smoke and manage thermal comfort. As yet these design features are not usually fully integrated with BIM technology but as simulation tools they are becoming more accessible through cloud computing and, more often than not, creating a new design facet and specialism which really should form part of the architectural design process during the architect's concept design stage. With the ability to generate much more manufacturing information the tendering manufacturers have a clearer insight as to what the building is, how the spaces are best arranged into modular units, what the science of the building consists of (together with all of the component equipment, pipe and cable runs, apertures in floors and walls, fixtures and fittings, and so on), all of which enable the design and manufacturing process to be more transparent and efficient.

CAD/CAM and Robotics

As CAD/CAM facilitates the design and construction of buildings in a conventional context it is also capable of playing a significant role in the manufacture of modular buildings, perhaps even more so. With the advent of automation in manufacturing becoming a prime candidate for manufacturers seeking to remain relevant, it is natural perhaps for robots to be considered in parallel as part of the modernization programme. As current levels of automation in manufacturing are an excellent partnership, so too

is robotics a natural fit, to a point where robots form the future in manufacturing automation.

The essence of manufacturing and assembling modular buildings is putting parts and components together, and assembly line robots occupy a zone between human involvement and total automation. An assembly robot has the capacity to operate faster with a superior degree of precision than a human and it is easily configured at will by a simple change in its programme. Assembly automation can include vision systems and force sensing which can guide a robot to execute specific tasks such as selecting a component from a conveyor and, with visual serving, allows the robot to rotate or translate one component to fit with another. Force sensing, on the other hand, provides feedback to the robot controller on aspects of how well the various parts are fitting together and how much force is being applied. Clearly the science behind robots in manufacturing is gathering pace by graduating from familiar tasks such as wielding a paint spray to embracing further levels of force control and machine vision. The robots' potential is widening to execute more refined tasks. The capacity for the robot to substitute for human involvement in undertaking simple repetitive tasks is under development to a point where human interaction in the actual manufacturing process can be reduced, necessitating the architect to design modular buildings accordingly.

The design of modular buildings in the age of robotic automation is a new challenge for architects where previous design conventions may need to be adjusted, if not abandoned altogether. In order for manufacturing to remain competitive and modular buildings desirable the architect will need to grasp the concepts of robotic automation processes. Just as in the recent past architects would formulate their detail designs based on a working understanding of what was reasonable and possible for the tradesperson to execute to an acceptable standard, so the same expectation will apply with regard to designing for the capacity of the robot. For example, a door or window detail would have been designed in a manner so that it can actually be built on the site, or a particular concrete detail would be formed in a sensible and economic way. Architectural design for modular buildings embracing robotic automation will be no different from the manner in which materials and components are assembled together by robots; it will be a process that should be part of the architectural design for robots to make in the first place. Where no architectural design input exists, the alternative is for the manufacturers and their team of robotic engineers to circumvent the art of architecture and focus on the production of an efficient manufacturing process, which undoubtedly it will.

Artificial Intelligence and Architecture

As the momentum surrounding robotic automation begins to increase within manufacturing environments the potential for artificial intelligence to function in parallel is also becoming a realization. The question surrounding the future design of modular buildings is: where might artificial intelligence (AI) begin and end in this process and under whose direction? Will robots be confined to the assembly function of parts and components only and be equipped with sufficient data to carry out efficient assembly activities, or is AI to evolve where the objective is for robots to actually design the parts and components too, and ultimately design the actual manner in which modular buildings are to be put together, just as an architect would do? That is, will AI become capable of producing site analysis in relation to its context, produce alternative plan layouts based on that analysis and be capable of factoring into a final design solution a myriad of other ingredients, features and characteristics normally associated with the function of an architect? Will the architecture and the aesthetics of modular buildings likewise be totally decided upon by the nature and extent of the data provided for robotic execution, and who might be best placed to decide on the intelligence of such data: an architect or a robotics engineer? These are questions requiring further

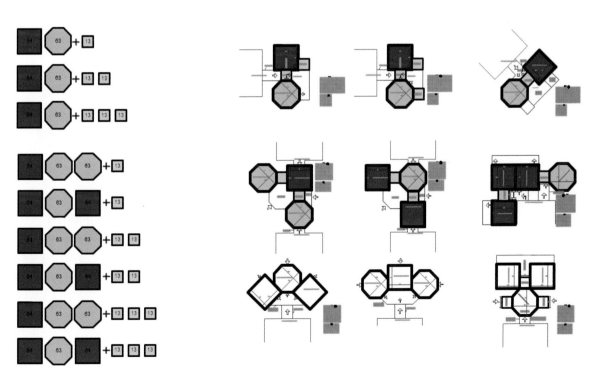

Optimal arrangement analysis for combinations of primary school teaching spaces. (Courtesy of HOCA Practice Research)

research but for now it might be sufficient to highlight the direction of travel for the design of modular buildings and where architects should be placed.

Clearly, architects and their profession generally are not yet up to speed or familiar with the design of components, their manufacture and assembly within modular buildings and what architectural design could bring to the scope of the modular building manufacture. Neither is the profession awash with project opportunities; smaller practitioners in particular are somewhat deprived of design opportunities and with the advent of robotic automation it would be easy for architects to become excluded from the process altogether. Design intelligence, however, is at the core of every architect's thinking, resulting from his/her training, experience and expertise. It is innate in architects how to analyse design problems, formulate concepts and produce solutions. Concepts for architects are a way of interpreting the brief and deciphering the options for designing a non-physical entity into a physical building, a reality incorporating and embracing numerous themes and emphases. It is the architect who has the skill and intelligence to understand the priority between the building's function and the aesthetic, depending on the nature and use of the building, and, at the same time, demonstrate innovativeness and flair. For AI to have meaning in the future of architectural design it should be influenced by a design intelligence founded on design principles and philosophies which inevitably will be influenced by the evolution of AI itself, hopefully under the scrutiny of the architect, but who in turn will also evolve as a consequence.

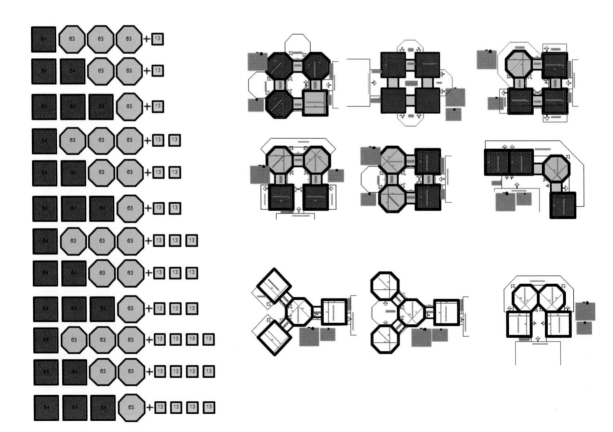

Teaching space arrangement analysis for individual school requirements, from a single classroom addition to a complete school. (Courtesy of HOCA Practice Research)

Chapter Seven

Features Common to Panelized and Modularized Buildings

Introduction

Within many sectors there is abundant scope for prefabricated buildings to validate the existence of both panel manufacturers and manufacturers of modular buildings for some time to come. As a complete turnkey solution, however, there is a greater interest evolving in modular buildings within various sectors other than housing. The future potential for modular buildings then, which is closely associated with expanding automation and eventually robotic assembly and artificial intelligence (AI), inevitably makes modular buildings a more obvious choice in substituting for many conventional construction practices.

A number of technical features surrounding prefabricated panelized and modularized buildings are common to both in terms of satisfying fire rating and acoustic requirements for instance, or airtightness and weathertightness perhaps, all of which are detailed and designed to incorporate their uniqueness. The potential for providing simple foundation solutions will apply to both, as will the choice of external cladding systems, but whilst on-site conditions will apply to panelized prefabrication this is not the case with modularized prefabrication where all internal and external finishes have the benefit of being fixed in a controlled factory environment.

There are, however, a number of features that are different between the two and which might need to be considered separately; for example, access restrictions might influence whether panelization is a more viable choice over modularization. Similarly, the overall advantages of manufacturing and assembly within a factory environment will clearly favour modularization more than panelization where complete turnkey solutions are preferred by many and almost unaffected by weather conditions.

From Factory to Site

Preparing the site for any building necessitates a series of investigations so as to understand what the site consists of, both above and below ground. On-site challenges above ground can be assessed more readily than those that exist below ground where, even with full investigations by way of trial holes or laser scanning, an element of risk will always prevail as 'unknowns' which might present themselves

Steel-framed modular unit being lifted from delivery vehicle into position as part of the final modular assemblage at the site location. (Courtesy of CIMC MBS Ltd)

during the course of the works. Analysing the site and minimizing risk is a key feature in every architect's design proposal.

Analysing the Site for Prefabricated Solutions

A natural element in any architectural design process is for the architect to visit the site and make observations as to the attributes and constraints associated with the site. There are obvious features such as trees that occupy land and space intended for new building which need to be investigated to establish whether any tree preservation orders (TPOs) might exist and to manage the same accordingly. Overhead cables, too, might need removing: depending on the nature of these cables, this may incur significant cost to the project. There are issues surrounding the boundary of the site which may influence the actual location of the building/s, such as the proximity of buildings on adjoining properties. The full extent of aspects which may, or may not, impact and influence the manner in which the architect's design process will progress for the site will vary according to its general context, its location, its orientation and a host of other features besides.

In addition to the above-ground features there are also features below ground necessitating a measure of detailed investigation, some of which might include soil contamination, below-ground cables or drains for connection purposes and even rivers or shifting sand which could influence foundation design, to name a few. Whilst the usual desktop studies and on-site trial holes will provide the architect with some initial indication as to the full extent of any unknown items, there will always remain a risk until the foundations are complete for the project. Where modular buildings have been decided upon as the preferred procurement route for the project from the outset, foundation design up to around six storeys tends to be less problematic compared to conventional building. Where options include a concrete slab foundation or helical piles an efficient

economical foundation is achievable. (*See* 'Technical Considerations' below.)

Accessing the Site for Logistics

Project viability includes the ease or difficulty with which the site can be accessed for the intended development where, in the first instance, satisfying planning requirements is usually a prerequisite. In undertaking a site analysis the architect will evaluate the features of the site, which includes a focus on the access points available from the public highway in order to assess the most suitable option for large vehicles. Clearly, a site that is located within a rural or suburban location might provide access to the site which is less problematic when compared to an urban or inner city location where different levels of access restrictions might apply for different vehicle types. Whilst the logistics associated with delivering panels to the site is a different prospect from delivering and lifting a fully fitted-out modular unit into position, the most challenging of lifts are very often overcome and simplified by the skill and expertise of the logistic personnel, whether within an inner city location or elsewhere. For example, lifting modular units from the public road over a two-storey house and into a rear garden location is not uncommon when under the management of experienced operators. Lifting a modular unit to first-floor level over an 80m reach is also possible for the experienced logistics team. The architect's site analysis and initial concept design process should allow for site personnel and vehicular traffic movements in and around the work-site itself and, as these are significant activities associated with all building projects, they must be handled and managed safely for whichever current health and safety rules apply.

The nature and extent of the site access will also inform the architect at concept design as to the largest volumetric modular unit size that can be used for the design of the modular buildings under consideration or if a combination of different size modular

Modular unit being lifted from the delivery lorry on the main road over a two-storey house and into position at the rear of the property.

Significantly larger modular unit consisting of a full-length rear addition being manoeuvred by mobile crane over the roof of the house from the main road. (Courtesy of Structural Timber Projects Ltd)

units would provide a more efficient result. Where restricted access prevents this, however, alternative solutions such as smaller modular units might provide a viable solution or panelization might offer the next viable alternative for delivering a design solution through prefabricated architecture. Knowing what is possible at RIBA Work Stage 0 (Strategic Definition and Strategic Brief), in particular, will inform the architect in how to make immediate and appropriate decisions affecting the Concept Design process, RIBA Work Stage 2.

Site Access

The architect should be sufficiently knowledgeable to form an opinion as to which of the two options would be more suitable for the nature of the site and its available access. Deciding on PAMA as the preferred procurement route up front as part of the initial Strategic Brief will focus on panelization or modularization. Panelization might form the whole of the superstructure at the site; alternatively, the project might consist of a total modular assemblage that is completed in a factory. The nature and extent of the available access to the site can vary somewhat and can impact in different ways for each of the two different prefabrication options. The selection process surrounding panelization or modularization as a viable alternative to a conventional build project will include accommodating any restrictions or limitations associated with the access and making any necessary adjustments accordingly.

Closed Panel Delivery

Where a panelized system is selected for the project the level of complexity is not too dissimilar to that of a conventional build project, and delivery vehicles tend to be much the same. Here too, the architect should be acquainted with how the panels are to be placed on the delivery vehicle for transportation and how they are lifted from the delivery lorry for installation into the building works and should design accordingly. The actual panel composition will dictate whether they are to be transported standing vertically or laid flat. Some manufacturers prefer to stack their closed panels vertically on cradles which are loaded at the factory and then lifted onto the lorry for delivery.

On arrival at the site the cradles are again lifted from the lorry to the preferred location at the site in readiness for the panels to be crane-lifted, as vertical components, directly from the cradle to their final positions within the building. This is especially appropriate for closed wall panels, where the structural integrity of the panel must not be compromised during the lifting process. The design size of the closed panel, whilst incorporating all the necessary features (such as thermal and acoustic properties, associated fire rating materials and so on), is also dictated by the building's storey height and by its length, which can vary according to the length of the preferred delivery lorry accessing the site. The weight of the closed panels is also to be considered as it will influence the size of the crane required on-site for lifting purposes. Equally significant is the

Closed panels stacked vertically on delivery cradle and being lifted into position within the building. (Photo by author)

reach required from the cradle location at the site to the panel's final fixed position within the building. The panel length is influenced more by the capacity of the delivery vehicle than by the ability of the manufacturer, although some manufacturers prefer to restrict the panel length to a maximum of 5m to suit convenient delivery or their particular manufacturing process or premises; the architect must design accordingly.

Open Panel Delivery

Open panels are usually placed flat on the delivery vehicle; the usual approach is for a consignment of open panels to be lifted on and off the vehicle in bundles and left in a convenient location on the site. From there the open panels are lifted into position one by one in a similar manner as the closed panels, usually by mobile crane although smaller cranes or other lifting equipment suitable for coping with the required weight, height and reach may be employed. It is usual for plant equipment to be used so as to comply with the current health and safety regulations and limitations associated with manhandling and lifting for operations at ground-floor level and above-ground level. The current edition of the Health and Safety Executive's publication *Manual Handling at Work* offers a brief guide and sets out what is expected of employers for their workers.

Structural Insulated Panels

Structural insulated panels (SIPs) are also delivered flat on the delivery vehicle and are in packs that are shrink-wrapped. When they arrive at the site, they should be stored flat, no more than sixteen panels high and over appropriate stillage to a slight fall so as to allow water run-off. Ideally, the SIPs and all associated timber rails, posts and splines should be stored inside or in dry sheltered conditions a minimum of 150mm off the ground level and kept covered with suitable polythene or tarpaulin until such time as the panels are required for installation. Because the width of the standard SIP is 1,220mm wide, arranging the loading on the lorry is done so as to prevent loads which overhang. Where the SIPs are already assembled into larger wall panel components the rules for their transportation are the same as for open and closed panel delivery.

Modular Buildings

Manufacturing modular buildings is dictated by a number of factors, some of which relate to the capacity of the manufacturer's factory facilities and in other instances it may be the restrictions and limitations imposed by allowable wide loads on UK roads. Designing modular buildings, therefore, requires the architect to possess a working knowledge and understanding of what rules and regulations exist and how the same will influence his/her design approach for their modular buildings by the size of the modular units which might be for a single house or a multi-house project, a multi-purpose hall or a health care building. The size of the modular units to be transported from the factory to the site location will determine whether the vehicle load is to be classified as normal or abnormal.

Lorries are permitted to carry certain weights and sizes depending on the vehicle. 'Normal loads' are those up to 44 tonnes, subject to axle restrictions. The length of certain vehicles is also limited, from 12m for a rigid vehicle to 18.65m for a road-train (a combination of a lorry and a trailer). It is the length of the trailer that is the variable whilst the width remains constant. The allowable width of 2.9m is often too narrow for many habitable space requirements and living preferences expected today but is often used for commercial applications or temporary accommodation. Modular units that exceed the allowable width on lorries are classified as 'abnormal loads'.

Abnormal loads are those where the modular unit overhangs the sides and/or rear of the trailer section of the vehicle. The requirements relating to transporting modular units that overhang at the rear and the sides are set out in the government's regulation 81 and 82 of the Road Vehicles (Construction and Use) Regulations; architects and clients should satisfy themselves that the appointed logistics company will undertake all transportation from the factory to the works site in accordance with all requirements that currently apply. It is, however, more usual for the manufacturer to undertake the transportation of the modular units and the responsibilities associated with the same. As part of the contract with the manufacturer, the appointment of a logistics company is normal practice as the latter will be well acquainted with what is required for compliance.

Optimum Design and Transportation

The ideal size for the actual modular unit becomes a principal feature of the architect's concept design process; s/he must be able to design modular units in a way that accords with the brief but which also makes the design and delivery process sensible, practical and cost-efficient. Some manufacturers prefer to manufacture a standard-width size with minimum, if any, customization and market their product accordingly, which also means minimum transportation issues. Others are more flexible and, indeed, in business to manufacture unit sizes to the architect's specific requirements or as one-off bespoke manufacture for a self-build client. Designing modular units beyond the standard 2.9m width constitutes an abnormal load and attracts additional provisions in transporting modular units to the site, some of which may necessitate escort provisions.

For a typical modular three-storey family house the width is clearly expected to be wider than 2.9m lest previously held perceptions surrounding 'prefab' are energized. For housing in particular it is the room width sizes that are the significant aspect for

the architect to remain mindful of as the length of the modular unit has greater flexibility for achieving the required room dimensions. It is more usual for houses to require room width sizes in excess of 2.9m; 4.2m is often a minimum but widths of 4.8m to 5.0m are naturally preferable and allow the architect to design spaces that are sensible and practical for residential purposes. The overhang on each side of the lorry, therefore, will equate to half of the difference between the width of the lorry at 2.9m and the overall width of the modular unit. The length of the modular unit, however, can vary to suit the particular modular building under design although it may not be longer than 18.65m, in which case the overhang will be on both the width and the rear of the lorry, depending on the length of the lorry selected.

Whilst a typical modular unit width size is normally around 2.9m wide overall and perhaps slightly wider in some cases, this is not conducive to good architectural design for residential space requirements. For example, the optimum size for a bedroom is around 4m × 4m and up to around 4.5m and wider if required, which allows sufficient space around a bed and for a sitting or dressing area within the room

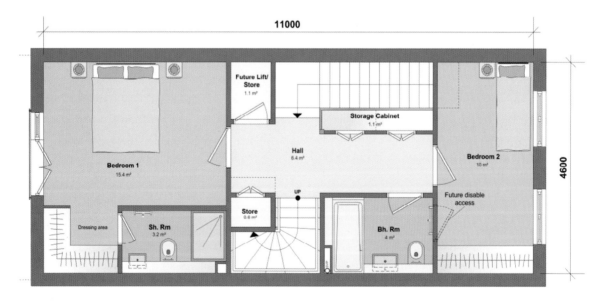

First-floor level plan for a three-storey family house 11m long and 4.6m wide: this will comfortably fit on the length of a delivery lorry but will generate an overhang at the sides. (Courtesy of HOCA Practice)

space, all of which is achievable within one single modular unit. Indeed, given the overall length of a modular unit that conveniently fits onto a lorry 18.65m or longer, a further bedroom and en suite is also achievable within the same modular unit.

Second bedrooms, children's bedrooms and ancillary spaces are often slightly smaller and economically arranged spaces can be achieved. Similarly, the ground-floor living arrangement can be conveniently accommodated within a single modular unit where the widest module forms the building's footprint. Additional space if required for the ground-floor module can be achieved by increasing its length, which does not create additional transport issues as a wide abnormal load will already necessitate an escort vehicle from the outset. Needless to say, not all modular buildings are for housing purposes but

the same modular design methodology is applied to modular apartment buildings where room sizes and living spaces are not too dissimilar. Moreover, sectors outside housing are also considered in a similar way where a full appreciation of the most optional modular unit size is a prerequisite for considering the most efficient design solution for the space arrangement required and at all times embracing all the attributes connected with premanufactured standardization.

Planning the Route, Abnormal Loads and Road Closures

A delivery vehicle laden with a completed volumetric unit must be able to negotiate a route to the site location from the factory. The vehicle must make its

Route planning at an early stage is an important element of any modular building project where low bridges, tight squeezes and difficult manoeuvring need to be avoided.

way very close to or perhaps onto the site to where the crane is located for lifting and final assembling into position. Options for placing panels or modular units on the delivery lorry will in turn dictate many other decisions: the size of the vehicle required; whether an over-sized load will necessitate an escort vehicle; what official notices need to be issued (well in advance) and approvals to be obtained; establishing the optimum route from the factory to the site to negate any minor roads where parked cars might obstruct access to the site; and which bridges are passable and which are to be avoided.

The preferred size for premanufacturing and delivering volumetric units is as large as possible so as to minimize the final number of modular units to be manufactured and thereby the number of lorry journeys from the factory to the site location. Anything above 18.65m and up to 27.4m long and above 3.0m and up to 5.0m wide is an abnormal load. That said, it is possible to transport modular units subject to

the required notices issued to the correct authorities and taking note of the time requirement for processes; the same applies where orders involving potential road closure for specific days at specific times might be involved. Other requirements have to be adhered to where the width of a particular road forming the route to the site has restricted use. Arranging the transportation of modular units is best left to the experts and the logistics team are best placed to undertake the overall responsibility for transportation and issuing the correct notifications. The costs associated with loads of this size should be evaluated against designing smaller modular units if the internal room dimensions will allow.

It is always prudent to arrange for the logistics team to be appointed well in advance of the actual delivery date. Planning the optimum route should be considered during the architect's concept design stage just like a desk-top study associated with the site conditions. There may be occasions and situations

Abnormal load with front escort.

where certain roads have to be used but which are a tight squeeze and others will need to be closed or partially closed for the duration of the site delivery process. For example, a particular local road may be the only viable option for the delivery lorry to access the site but may have parking on both sides. Where a relatively small number of modular units are involved the road closure can be confined to a small block of time or perhaps the modular units can be agreed to be delivered over a weekend period. For larger modular buildings, and of significant number to matter, a certain amount of project planning and coordination is called for. Thus, depending on the size of the project and where a certain number of modular units have to be delivered each day for a period of weeks or even months, the road closure arrangements are a vital element of the project planning and a period of eight to ten weeks minimum needs to be allowed for to ensure the correct consents and approvals are in place and all necessary documents obtained well in advance of the delivery process.

Whilst the practicalities and logistics of the site management are ultimately the domain of the main contractor or the manufacturer perhaps, the initial design considerations falls to the architect. Within the architect's concept design process where scrutiny of design ideas is tested, s/he is expected to have a good understanding and appreciation of the site on which the building's footprint will be sited if the building's design is to be realized. Allied to this understanding are the sizes of the various modular units designed for the project and the ability for delivery vehicles to deliver the same from the factory to the work site. The nature and extent of the access to the site are crucial therefore, where sufficiently wide access and turning ability, either off-site or on-site, are called for. Other constraints which impede access, off-loading and installation around the site may revolve around the site's physical boundaries, proximity of adjoining buildings, imposition of trees to be retained, overhead cables and similar features. Factors such as these dictate and influence the manner in which a single or large modular building is designed and assembled

at the site location and has to be designed and manufactured accordingly.

Technical Considerations

Foundation Types and Preparation

The word 'foundation' is applied to numerous situations to define specific meaning relating to the subject matter under discussion. For example, in an educational context an individual may be described as lacking the foundation necessary to undertake advanced study, or 'foundation' might apply to the basis upon which something or a proposition is grounded; for example, 'there is no foundation for such objection'. Within the context of a building, however, its meaning is specific: a foundation forms the lowest support of a structure and may be built on top of solid rock or on various types of soil. The sole purpose of foundations is to transfer the loads imposed by the superstructure to the soil below. The composition of soil can vary on sites depending on location and its characteristics are a very important feature. The nature of the soil's particles, their size, density and structural properties are identified from the soil tests which are carried out to inform the design process for all building projects and the foundations are designed accordingly. The nature and extent of the foundations required for a building's superstructure are informed by the nature of the ground-bearing capacity that exists within the soil and the load of the building intended for the location on the site.

Prefabricated and modular buildings do not always necessitate the foundations normally associated with conventional build projects as the weight of the superstructure is generally lighter than that of a conventional masonry building. There are a number of ready-made foundation options available to accommodate both temporary prefabricated buildings and prefabricated buildings intended to remain as more permanent structures. They vary

Pad foundations consisting of regular precast concrete paving slabs are often used for temporary modular building locations. (Photo by author)

from simple surface-mounted and shallow pad foundations to shallow foundations (sometimes referred to as footings) to deep foundations. Surface-mounted or shallow pad foundations will suffice where the loads of the building are low to the bearing capacity of the soils and are often employed for single-, two- and three-storey prefabricated buildings.

Trench Foundations

If the loadings imposed by the building are not adequately supported by the surface soils they will have to be transferred to a deeper level where the soil layers have a higher bearing capacity; for this a deep foundation is usually employed. Deep foundations are formed by digging out a continuous trench to a prescribed width and depth and laying a layer of concrete to form a 'footing' to a prescribed thickness at the bottom which, when properly cured, allows the rising walls to be built up to ground level in brickwork or blockwork. In some cases, the rising brick

or block walls are abandoned and instead are substituted by filling the complete width of the trench with concrete, hence 'trench foundations'. This is often a more economical approach as the cost and time required for brick- and block-laying (as compared to a continuous concrete pour as a single operation) are often more favourable as the time requirement is reduced considerably.

Raft Foundations

A raft is a reinforced concrete slab, often referred to as 'raft foundations', which functions by distributing the load of the building's walls or any point loads such as columns over its area and this often provides a fast and efficient foundation solution. By spreading the loads of the building's superstructure in this way the concrete raft floats over the ground like a timber raft would float on top of water. A raft foundation is an ideal solution for prefabricated buildings as it is a very convenient and expedient

Concrete raft foundation occupies the total footprint of the building with perimeters profiled below to accommodate the wall loadings.

solution for getting out of the ground quickly and allowing the building's superstructure to commence in a timely fashion. The depth of a raft can be kept to 140mm thick with the reinforcement increased accordingly, which is convenient for minimizing the dig into the ground and not having to dispose of unwanted earth, some of which may also be contaminated, which has a higher cost implication. The raft occupies the total footprint of the building and the perimeter profile can be designed to accommodate a brick plinth detail or the preferred fixing detail for either a panelized or modularized building. Where an issue with underground services or contaminated soils exists, a raft is a very effective and economical way of avoiding disturbance to the ground below.

Pile Foundations

Beyond the more obvious foundation options referred to earlier where most tend to apply to residential building projects, there are ground conditions where piling might prove to be a more appropriate solution for the ground conditions. Piling solutions tend to be used where the composition of the soil at the upper levels of the ground are incapable of preventing abnormal settlement or resist uplift. Pile foundations are often used for large building structures beyond the scale of housing developments.

There are a variety of piling solutions available for the many different ground conditions and situations which can be found in different sites. They range from bored piles, mini-bored piles to driven piles (hammered), from sheet piles to friction piles, and the appropriateness of each piling option relative to the ground conditions is usually decided by the professional design team following the design analysis carried out by the structural engineer. The final choice of piling may be influenced by factors other than the bearing capacity of the ground, such as the location of the site within a sensitive area where driven piles would be less favourable as compared to bored piles (a less noisy operation), for example. The architect and the professional team will undertake a proper analysis of the site and the ground conditions which prevail and are always best placed, therefore, to provide the most appropriate foundation solution for any given situation having explored cost comparisons, site access, disruption, time implications and the host of other considerations normally associated with such an exercise.

Prefabricated buildings do not normally necessitate heavily engineered foundations and whilst surface-mounted pad foundations are often used for temporary prefabricated buildings, permanent prefabricated buildings require a different approach for panelized and modularized solutions. In order to maintain efficiencies surrounding the cost and time savings associated with prefabricated buildings, the potential for minimizing work activities relating to foundations is always considered to be a win-win situation. Substituting typical concrete foundations and excavations with a simple screw pile installation is a favourable option.

A screw pile foundation is not unlike a bored pile application except the pile does not require a steel reinforcement cage and concrete in the bore formed by heavy plant equipment such as an auger. Each screw pile section, sometimes referred to as a helical pile, is a steel tube of a given length, usually around 2–3m long, with a helix at the bottom end to enable the steel pile to be wound (screwed) into the ground. A screw pile for the whole of its total length in the ground can have more than one helix, the number being dictated by the nature of the ground and its bearing capacity for the intended load of the building. A screw pile can also have a number of sections and for every 2–3m depth required an additional pile section is added until the required bearing capacity is achieved. The top of the screw pile, therefore, is designed to take additional lengths of steel pile tubes so as to screw the bottom of the helix to the required designed depth and bearing pressure. Screw piles can be inserted into the ground to a depth of 30m (approximately 100ft) and can vary in diameter from

100mm (which normally applies to residential and domestic-scale buildings) up to 300mm (which is suitable for the loadings demanded by larger and industrial applications).

Once the correct depth and ground-bearing pressure are achieved (established by the machine operator at the time of installation), the top of the steel screw pile is capped off with a metal plate upon which the ground beams are fixed to suit the design of the prefabricated superstructure. Alternatively, floor cassettes designed for panelized buildings include ground beams to span between the pile cap positions, which allow for the ground-floor installation to be completed very rapidly ready for

First 3m section of helical pile is presented to the position marked out on the ground, with verticality constantly monitored by the operator of the piling machine. (Courtesy of TMP UK South Ltd, photo by author)

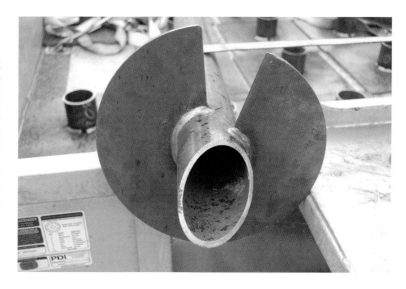

Helix located at the bottom of the first pile section, with an additional helix added to each additional pile section as required to achieve the correct bearing pressure. (Courtesy of TMP UK South Ltd, photo by author)

True vertical alignment is constantly maintained throughout the entire piling process with checks at regular intervals. (Courtesy of TMP UK South Ltd, photo by author)

the immediate erection of the wall panels. Modular buildings usually accommodate the ground-floor spanning and loading requirements within the floor structure of the modular unit. Consequently, the ability to position each corner and central positions of a modular unit on top of a screw pile makes an attractive proposition for a modular building project.

Installing screw pile foundations is a simple and exceptionally speedy operation, often requiring only one or two persons to set up and operate a single-piece plant which varies in size according to the diameter size of the pile required. Once the precise locations for the pile are established on the ground the piles are installed by the machine at regular centres to the structural engineer's design, maintaining verticality of the pile throughout the process. Because the installation process is very quick the time necessary to prepare the site for a modular building is reflected in the overall time required to design, manufacture and assemble a modular building at the site location. Also, minimum disruption is caused to adjoining properties and minimum disturbance is caused to the ground as the normal plant and vehicle movements in and around the site are reduced considerably by eliminating foundation excavations and pouring of concrete.

Timely Design Decisions

Project at the Crossroads

Very often prefabrication is only examined as an option well after the concept design is completed. Very often too, the detail design originally intended for a conventional build project is well advanced. Endeavours to shoehorn prefabrication into a building previously designed for a conventional build process usually produces very disappointing results and does little if anything to move the project out of intensive care. Substitutions of this nature well into the procurement process tend to focus on panelization as opposed to modularization as a more viable option where the objective might be solely to reduce construction costs or to retrieve some of the time lost by non- or late decision-making, or both, at the front end of the project.

Regretfully, in too many cases the prefabrication options are only examined well after RIBA Work Stage 0 (Strategic Decisions) and Work Stage 1 (Preparation and Brief) and often after concept design is completed at Work Stage 2, as opposed to being part of the architect's initial design considerations. Very often too, for these community-type projects the detail design might be well advanced or perhaps completed for what was originally intended to be a conventional building. The nature of the contract between the contractor and the client will highlight even further the practicalities of making changes, which in some cases may be totally prohibitive from the outset due to charges the contractor may be entitled to under the contract. This state of affairs might be more prevalent for community-related projects such as education, health, housing and so on. In the private sector, however, the necessity for making strategic decisions early produces a clearer focus and purpose; consequently, the decision-making process does not come under the political influence, local strategies, timing and budget issues as may be the case within the public sector.

Making any design changes will have a negative impact on the overall well-being of the project as intensive changes at a late stage tend to be undertaken in a hurry and, where exhaustive time is necessary to verify the viability of proposed changes, it can sometimes negate any cost or time benefit being sought. Equally, the amount of abortive design work for the architect and other design team professionals can also be a significant extra cost; this is an element which is usually overlooked or in some cases not even considered but which can also become a problematic issue if payment is not forthcoming to the design team, thereby obliging the architect on some occasions to apply a greater focus on other project committments.

Panelization is often considered to be a viable option compared to modularization, whereas modularization is a totally different concept and procurement process for delivering buildings and would necessitate a full redesign from the beginning. Substituting selected elements of conventional build with panelization, though, will still spawn some new questions; namely, which type of panelization is appropriate as a substitute, given the status of the project and design process, and what are the potential cost and time savings to be achieved, if any? In circumstances such as these the SIPS option would be a good choice on the basis that manufacturing time is not unreasonable and the better manufacturers are already organized with a list of approved partners who are equipped to undertake the necessary installation. The potential response is more immediate with a SIPS solution when compared to closed panel if compared on a like-for-like basis. The SIPS option forms an instant structural wall solution which is already insulated which, when the installation is complete, allows both the external cladding and internal fit-out to be carried out in parallel; this is where time can be recouped. The scope for simplifying the foundations design using a panelized solution also exists although there is no significant difference when comparing closed panel to an SIPS.

Understanding the physical composition of the panel components is a fundamental criterion for the architect, especially where standard-size panels are to be applied to the maximum such as SIPS. Where a part or the whole of the building is to be substituted with panelization the architect will be required to make speedy changes to the detail design process which will attract a further design fee and which should also form a part of the overall project value engineering process.

The same will apply to a redesign for substituting a previously designed conventional building with a modular building design but which will require some additional time to make the necessary changes. Of course where a total overhaul of the project is identified as necessary or deemed to be the most appropriate course of action to adopt, the option for a modular building solution presents some attractive opportunities for cost savings more than time savings but where the client indicates more time exists than funding, the former usually takes precedent.

Impact of Changes

Instigating design change during or after the sign-off of the RIBA Work Stage 3 (Developed Design) or, worse still, Work Stage 4 (Technical Design) will have the greatest negative impact on the project and any aspiration to achieve cost or time savings through value engineering are diminished accordingly. For the viability of a project to be interrogated at such a late stage would suggest the quality of the cost analysis carried out at the initial stages of the project was less than robust or that some serious event/s occurred or project risk/s transpired later which were not adequately costed or that insufficient time was allowed for in the original project timeline. On the other hand, it is unreasonable for a client to expect absolute cost certainty from day one as if the project can be treated like a mathematical calculation. Where an element of remodelling forms part of the project and potential below-ground risks lurk, in addition to any implications associated with satisfying planning conditions and building control, there is always risk. Procuring a building, irrespective of its size and nature, commercial or domestic, is not an exact science and where risks prevail a contingency sum is usually allowed for in the contract which should be in line with the known risks at least.

Changing from a conventional designed building to a modular building might mean a change in the planning consent already obtained. Should this be the case a new modular building design might necessitate a minor change, a material change or even a totally new planning application, given that the expectation for the finished materials of the building is usually the norm for creating savings. The cost associated with changing from a conventional building to a prefabricated alternative and the time impact a delay will have on the project might not justify considering changing in the first place. Assessing the project for a prefabricated design solution from the very beginning and for the same to be at least assessed for viability at RIBA Work Stages 0 and 1 is almost obligatory but not later during the Concept Design stage has been demonstrated to be a prudent decision. For the client to embark on these value engineering explorations, however, s/he would be well advised to arrive at a very swift decision on whether to proceed with the building project as originally designed or not, lest the risk of not succeeding is the only result to be achieved but where additional time lost is the only certainty.

Certified Approvals

Whilst there are numerous manufacturers capable of producing panelized products as part of the on-site construction process and modular buildings as a complete turnkey system, there are some manufacturers who do not enjoy the benefit of a formal certificated status. Certification is a very important ingredient and confirms a mark of excellence ensuring the prefabricated products used either as components or as a building system are safe, are of high quality and reliable and, especially, are regulatory-compliant. The British Board of Agrément (BBA) is a recognized UK body which provides certification for prefabricated products and systems in buildings, but they are not the only industry body offering accreditation for prefabricated and modular buildings. As a third-party organization they undertake structural and integrity testing, performance and durability testing, conformance and fitness for purpose testing of the manufacturer's products and systems and will certify accordingly. The standard building height for prefabricated panelized structures to be accredited is generally four storeys. More recently, however, certain prefabricated systems have gained accreditation for buildings to a height of six storeys and with advances in manufacturing technology further building heights are being examined. Manufacturers who have attained such standards possess a product or system recognized by professional consultants, local authority building control, approved inspectors, building insurers and trades organizations.

Whilst self-builders will be interested in standards and certification associated with the products and materials they are proposing to use, developers and contractors will also have a focus on the completed building, whether it is a school, sports centre, commercial building or housing. Warranties are of particular interest to the prospective house buyer and developer who seek assurance with a guarantee that the housing provided will meet prescribed standards. In order to be able to sell their houses and apartments the housing development offered to the market is registered with one of the housing guarantee schemes offered by NHBC, BOPAS, Premier and the like. NHBC is a well-known organization whose focus is founded on providing a BuildMark status which is a ten-year warranty policy to the house buyer where the NHBC-registered builder has registered a conventional on-site build project. For the past two years in particular the NHBC have also become more alert to the changing market in relation to off-site manufacturing (OSM) whereby they will now assess off-site manufactured panelized and modular systems for compliance with their existing warranty embracing their current NHBC standards for conventional build processes.

Panelized and modular building has a much shorter history compared to conventional construction in terms of warranties and guarantees being available for the homeowner. Indeed, due to the absence of available warranties it has been a significant obstacle for many house builders and manufacturers seeking to promote the development of prefabricated and modular home building as a viable alternative to conventional build practices. Technology and automation have advanced significantly in relation to premanufactured modular building, however, and so too has the urgency in providing homes at a quicker pace, which together make accreditation more justified. As a consequence of this significant state in the housing market new players in the housing warranty guarantee business have materialized. BOPAS and Premier are companies recognized as major players who offer manufacturers of modular homes a guarantee scheme something akin to that for conventional on-site house construction.

As with conventional build projects, prefabricated and modular buildings can secure accreditation with assurance of integrity for a manufacturing system demonstrating consistency, competency and quality which adhere to prescribed specifications. Recognized and approved bodies assess all aspects relating to the manufacturer's business operation, their processes and procedures. They examine the coordination of design with manufacturing and assembly through to the final assembly at the site location. Procedures in handover to the client are assessed and evaluated, as are issues surrounding changes to the project and matters associated with alleviating delivery risk. As technology, architectural design and manufacturing continue to evolve so too will the providers of warranty and guarantee schemes need to keep pace. Prefabricated and modular building practice and procedures that adhere to the required design and manufacturing standards will allow builders, developers and manufacturers access to immediate and automatic verification for mortgage finance purposes. Warranty and guarantee schemes relating to manufactured for PAMA are as robust as those applied to conventional build and it is incumbent upon the self-builder, home buyer and developer alike to satisfy themselves as to the appropriateness of the same for their specific purpose.

THE UK HAS HAD A LONG JOURNEY IN prefabrication since the period immediately after the Second World War when, under the Housing Act, the Ministry of Works was tasked with addressing the acute housing shortage. Prefabrication was identified then as a means for replacing some of the homes lost as a result of the hostilities. Although a total of 156,623 temporary prefabricated houses were built during the period 1945–51 the negative aspects of this endeavour appear to remain. Moreover, with the introduction of the large panel system (LPS) during the 1960s the urban environment was also blighted by the ubiquitous tower blocks displaying acres of concrete of a repetitive nature. It was perhaps the tragedy at Ronan Point, together with the recognition of the demolition of community and the social fabric that the tower blocks represented, that prompted society, politicians and planners to find alternative solutions.

Housing shortages have never been resolved but the enthusiasm for creating family housing more connected to the ground level appeared to have been given a new lease of life. With this new impetus in place a steady supply of new-build family houses and low-rise apartments appeared to meet housing demands. It was not until the economic crash in 2008 that the focus on conventional building became a subject for scrutiny. It is not fully explained whether it was a sudden scarcity of money or that conventional construction was deemed to be too slow to meet the growth in demand which had been gathering significant pace since the early 2000s. However, from the early 2000s a focus was suddenly placed on alternatives to conventional construction and prefabrication

was once again a subject for discussion, although under a new guise of off-site manufacturing (OSM).

Needless to say, where opportunity opens up the industrial entrepreneur will seek to occupy that space, resulting in significant numbers of off-site manufacturers entering the market. Primarily, the manufacture of wall panels was identified as a substitute for part of the conventional construction process, with a selection of open and closed wall panel components. Certainly, the concept had a measure of momentum, especially in relation to substituting the hitherto slow labour-intensive handcraft trades associated with conventional construction. Suddenly mechanization, factory efficiency, cleaner working environments, health and safety, quality in finishes and a host of other buzzwords and expressions gathered a degree of momentum to a point where OSM itself is now becoming somewhat superseded with terminology such as full automation, robotic assembly, artificial intelligence and robotic machine learning.

What is perhaps ominous is the demise of the traditional construction methods and practices; the quest for efficiencies in cost and in time remain omnipresent but perhaps have greater urgency. The market for new housing as well as in other community sectors will always exist in sufficient volume to justify the existence of the small building company as well as the larger consortiums. Companies with sufficient resources are already grasping the opportunity to switch their focus from conventional house building to manufacturing their own modular buildings where the vision of volume mass production provides attractive balance sheets. The manufacturing fraternity already engaged in wall panel production, and more of late in manufacturing modular house and apartment buildings, tends not to be fully geared up to undertake larger modular building projects (as in the Croydon example) or the huge volume unit low-rise housing projects often spoken about. The irony is that whereas the industrialist in the early 1920s took hold of the opportunity to enter the construction business, some large construction companies today are turning their hand to manufacturing.

The government has for some time been advocating the need for mass housing using modern methods of construction without recognizing that the present state of individual OSM industry is perhaps ill-equipped to undertake mass housing projects. Notwithstanding, many existing manufacturers are indeed capable of delivering small to medium-size housing projects but are excluded perhaps on the basis that government procurement officials are not convinced that they are achieving the best value for money or economies of scale. Their preference (until the time of Carillion) appeared to be invested in a selected number of only large construction companies but since the demise of Carillion not much effort, if any, has been employed in spreading risk by distributing some projects among smaller companies. Perhaps the government is biding its time until the new large construction industrialists are fully geared up.

Amid all the enthusiasm associated with prefabricated and modular architecture and the future prospects associated with existing manufacturers and aspiring new industrialists, there is little mention, if any, of where the architect and the profession might engage. As the scope for growth in prefabrication and modular buildings gathers new momentum, a huge void exists surrounding architectural design. The emphasis naturally is largely placed on manufacturing and assembly techniques, as indeed it should, but one would hope not in isolation of architectural intelligence and input lest we arrive again at results where negative perceptions will have new perspective and meaning. There is no doubt the appetite for premanufactured modular buildings prevails unabated, but it is for the architect's profession to make more imposing gestures involving PAMA as it evolves. This is not just to ensure the well-being of the environment for which the architect has a responsibility but also to ensure architectural design excellence is upheld more than the architect merely having a presence on the sidelines.

As prefabricated and modular architecture takes its place within the urban and rural environment, so the process necessitates engagement with planning officials and interested parties who also foster the best interests for the built environment. Whilst a long history exists for insisting new development must coincide with references of significance and value, some leeway has to be granted now with regard to the new science of building. It has to be recognized that architectural design for premanufactured buildings which inevitably will be executed in a factory, eventually by robot assembly processes, will necessitate a different culture in architectural detailing. It is less than reasonable to expect and insist that the architectural design of premanufactured buildings must adhere to traditional brick-built styles and cultural values of a totally historic nature; it negates the contribution to manufacturing science that AI has to offer in the new art of architecture. The overriding point to highlight, therefore, is the importance of architects engaging at the front end of the manufacturing process where architectural design provides the catalyst for superior manufacturing quality, both in terms of design and manufacture. It is important, therefore, for the architect to train the robot in architectural design as part of the machine learning process and not be subjected to the results a self-taught robot might produce.

However, current thinking appears to indicate a new mood of expectation where high-performance machine automation and robotic assembly, even robotic design through machine learning, will become instrumental in manufacturing buildings based on architectural design principles as opposed to constructing them in the conventional way.

Anderson, M. and Anderson, P. (2007). *Prefab Prototypes: Site-Specific Design for Offsite Construction*. Princeton Architectural Press, New York.

Bew, M. (2018). House of Lords Select Committee on Science and Technology, Corrected Oral Evidence: Off-Site Manufacture for Construction. Available at http://data.parliament.uk/writtenevidence/committeeevidence.svc/evidencedocument/science-and-technology-committee-lords/offsite-manufacture-for-construction/oral/82495.html (accessed September 2018).

Bourke, K., Clift, M., Garvin, S., Harrison, H. and Trotman, P. (2007). *Designing Quality Buildings: A BRE Guide*. IHS BRE Press, Watford, UK.

Brunskill, R.W. (2000). *Vernacular Architecture: An Illustrated Handbook*. Faber & Faber, London.

Department for Business, Energy and Industrial Strategy (2018). Response to House of Lords Science and Technology Select Committee (2017–19), 2nd Report of Session, Off-Site Manufacture for Construction: Building for Change. Available at https://www.parliament.uk/documents/lords-committees/science-technology/off-site-manufacture-for-construction/Govt-response-off-site-manufacture-construction.pdf

Ford, A. (2007). *Designing the Sustainable School*. Images Publishing, Victoria, Australia.

Goodman, A. (2017). Making Prefabrication American: The Work of A. Lawrence Kocher, *Journal of Architectural Education* 71 (1), pp. 22–33, DOI:10.1080/10464883.2017.1260916.

House of Lords (2017–19). Science and Technology Select Committee, 2nd Report of Session, Off-Site Manufacturing for Construction: Building for Change. HL Paper 169. Available at publications.parliament.uk/pa/ld201719/ldselect/ldstech/169/16902.htm

Johnson, N.J. and Giorgis, C. (2002). Children's Books: Technology. *The Reading Teacher* 55 (7), pp. 696–704.

Joye, Y. (2007). Fractal Architecture Could Be Good for You. *Nexus Network Journal* 9, pp. 311–20. Available at http://doi.org/10.1007/s00004-007-0045-y

Knapp, C. (2013). Why It's Time to Give Up on Prefab. Retrieved from https://www.archdaily.com/453236/why-it-s-time-to-give-up-on-prefab

Leopold, C. (2006). Geometry Concepts in Architectural Design, in Proceedings of the 12th International Conference on Geometry and Graphics, ISGG 6–10 August, 2006, Salvador, Brazil: ISGG. Lo Turco, M., & Sanna, M. (2010).

McKinsey & Company (2017). Reinventing Construction: A Route to Higher Productivity. Retrieved from https://www.mckinsey.com/~/media/McKinsey/Industries/Capital%20Projects%20and%20Infrastructure/Our%20Insights/Reinventing%20construction%20through%20a%20productivity%20revolution/MGI-Reinventing-construction-A-route-to-higher-productivity-Full-report.ashx

Mandelbrot, B. (1975). *The Fractal Geometry of Nature*. Henry Holt & Co., New York.

Melbourne School of Design (2011). *Future Proofing Schools*. Brochure 4 Prefabrication.

Roland Berger Report (2018). Prefabricated Housing Market in Central and Northern Europe: Overview of Market Trends and Development. Retrieved from https://www.rolandberger.com/en/Publications/Prefabricated-housing-market.html

Roth, L.M. (1983). America Builds: Source Documents in American Architecture and Planning. Harper & Row. Available at https://www.goodreads.com/book/show/1200354.America_Builds

Ross, D. and Britain Express (2011). Retrieved from http://www.britainexpress.com/History

Salingaros, N.A. (2008). *A Theory of Architecture*. UMBAU-VERLAG Harald Puschel, Solingen, Germany.

Salingaros, N.A. and Tejada, D.M. (2001). Modularity and the Number of Design Choices. *Nexus Network Journal* 3 (1), pp. 99–109.

Salingaros, N.A. and West, B.J. (1999). A Universal Rule for the Distribution of Sizes. *Environment and Planning B: Planning and Design* 26, pp. 909–923.

Sebestyén, G. (1998). *Construction: Craft to Industry*. E. & F.N. Spon, London.

Smith, P.F. (2003). *The Dynamics of Delight: Architecture and Aesthetics*. Routledge, New York.

Smith, R.E. (2010). *Prefab Architecture: A Guide to Modular Design and Construction*. John Wiley & Sons, Hoboken, New Jersey.

Staib, G., Dorrhofer, A. and Rosenthal, M. (2008). *Components and Systems: Modular Construction*. Birkhäuser, Basel.

Taylor, M.D., Fisher, A. and Wamuziri, S. (2009). A Comparison of Modern Methods of Bathroom Construction: A Project Case Study. Retrieved from http://www.arcom.ac.uk/-docs/proceedings/ar2009-1173-1182_Taylor_Fisher_and_Wamuziri.pdf

Ung, T. (2018). Three Tiers of Prefabrication. Available at https://journeyofanarchitect.com/blog/three-tiers-of-prefabrication (accessed November 2019).

Vale, B. (1996). *Prefabs: The History of the UK Temporary Housing Programme*. E. & F.N. Spon, London.

AI artificial intelligence

AIROH Aircraft Industries Research Organisation on Housing

BBA British Board of Agrément

BIM building information modelling

BOPAS Buildoffsite Property Assurance Scheme

BREEAM Building Research Establishment Environmental Assessment Method

CAD computer aided design

CAE computer aided engineering

CAM computer aided manufacture

CIOB Chartered Institute of Builders

CNC computer numerical control

DFA design for assembly

DFM design for manufacture

DfMA designing for manufacture and assembly

LPS large panel system

MMC modern methods of construction

NHBC National House Building Council

OSB oriented strand board

OSM off-site manufacturing

PAMA prefabricated and modular architecture

PS polystyrene

PUR polyurethane rigid

SIP structural insulated panel

SIPS structural insulated panel [building] system

SECO Selection Engineering Company Ltd